I0819549

Happy Plants

DISCLAIMER

This book is a reference book about the history of plants and their uses, the information in this book is for informational purposes only and any recipes within it are for reference purposes only. You should not use, follow or make any of the recipes in this book or encourage others to do so. This book is not intended as a replacement for professional medical treatment and should not be relied upon as recommending, encouraging or promoting any specific diet or practice. It is also not intended as a guide to which plants are edible or have nutritional or medicinal benefits or to replace the advice of a nutritionist, physician or medical practitioner.

We strongly advise you to consult a medical practitioner before using any herbal remedies, especially if you have an existing medical condition, are taking medication, are pregnant or are breast-feeding. You should not use the information in this book as a substitute for diagnosis, medication or other treatment prescribed by your medical practitioner.

There is the possibility of allergic or other adverse reactions from the use of any plants mentioned (and plants not mentioned) in this book. You should seek the advice of your doctor or other qualified health provider with any questions you may have, especially in relation to medical conditions or allergies. Some plants may interact with prescription drugs including, but not limited to, the Pill and anti-depressants; if you are using any medication you should always consult with a qualified medial practitioner before taking any herbal remedies.

The publishers and author do not accept any liability for any harm that results from your use, or misuse, of this book, or for your failure to seek appropriate medical advice.

Happy Plants

100 things to grow to make you smile, and how to make them happy too

ZIA ALLAWAY

Contents

Introduction

Most of us know instinctively that plants make us happy. The joy we feel when given a bouquet of colourful blooms or the positive energy we experience when walking through a wood or meadow dotted with wild flowers is undeniable, but you may be wondering why plants have these effects.

This book aims to answer that question, delving into the science that explains how flowers can focus our minds and help our brains recharge, and why the scent of our favourite plants can stimulate happy memories. It also explores the reasons why some colours help us to relax and enjoy the moment and how the antics of bees and birds that visit our garden plants also bring joy.

More surprising, perhaps, are the plants that provide environmental benefits above and beyond their well-documented power to reduce carbon emissions by absorbing CO_2. Did you know, for instance, that sunflowers can help to clean up soils contaminated with dangerous heavy metals, or that some everyday hedging plants can trap the small air particles in vehicle exhaust emissions, reducing pollution levels? These fascinating facts and more are revealed in the pages that follow.

Herbs and edibles offer us tasty treats that make us smile, but many also deliver a range of amazing health benefits, boosting our immunity and helping to ward off heart disease, some cancers, and Type 2 diabetes. The good news is that nutrient-rich plants with these special powers such as tomatoes and chillies are easy to grow in a pot on a balcony or terrace.

Other plants, including many that we use to decorate our homes, make us happy because their natural shape and colour lifts our mood with their natural grace and beauty.

The evidence is all there to prove that plants make us happy on a number of different levels, and by selecting a few of your favourites, you can reap the benefits, whether you have a windowsill, small patio, town garden, or an acre of land to grow them on.

Positive plants

Most plants have the power to boost our mental wellbeing and make us happy, but this selection is particularly beneficial, and planting a few in your garden will help to bring you joy throughout the year.

Japanese maple

ACER PALMATUM

Benefits
Foliage interest; autumn colour; interesting seed heads; wildlife plant (food for birds and moth caterpillars)

Height & spread
From 2.5 x 2.5m (8 x 8ft) to 4 x 4m (13 x 13ft) or more, depending on the cultivar

One of the most popular trees for small gardens, the colourful Japanese maple will bring a smile to your face all year round, but its spectacular autumn show, when the leaves sparkle in shades of red, crimson, orange and yellow, marks it out from the crowd.

The sheer elegance and beauty of maple trees will improve your mood, capturing your attention as they evolve with each passing season, and helping your brain to switch off and relax. Children also enjoy collecting the fiery autumn leaves and making them into colourful collages or acer bunting by stringing them together. The tree produces winged seed cases just before leaf fall, too, which spin in the air like tiny helicopters, gripping the imagination of adults and children alike.

The benefits continue throughout winter, when the patterns made by the now-visible branches also hold our attention. Studies show that these repetitive patterns, known as fractals, hold our gaze yet are easy for our minds to process, allowing the brain to recover from stress.

There are over a thousand varieties of *Acer palmatum* to choose from, each sporting this maple's distinctive finely cut, hand-shaped foliage in various forms and sizes. Beginners may wish to opt for one with simple lobed leaves, such as 'Ōsakazuki', 'Sango-kaku', and the moody purple 'Bloodgood', which tend to be more tolerant of a range of site and soil conditions. 'Sango-kaku' also sports coral-coloured new shoots in spring, while the compact cultivar 'Winter Flame' has pink-tinged young shoots and pinky red bark through winter. Trees that offer this additional stem interest are known as coral bark maples.

All Japanese maples prefer a sheltered location in partial shade, with moist but free-draining soil.

Snapdragon

ANTIRRHINUM

Benefits
Scented flowers; good cut flower; pollinator plant; wildlife plant (food for birds)

Height & spread
90 x 30cm (36 x 12in) for tall varieties; shorter cultivars are also available

These timeless annual flowers with their intriguing summer blooms have been favourites for many generations, and may have been enjoyed by your grandparents and great-grandparents in their gardens.

Deservedly popular, snapdragons come in a vast array of colours, from fiery red and dark burgundy to pale pink and elegant white, but it is their curiously constructed flowers that set them apart from other bedding plants and make us happy.

Gently squeeze the outer edges of the tubular flowers and they open their dragon-like mouths to reveal the nectar and pollen inside. While this is a great game for children, bees cottoned on to it long before us humans, and you can watch them clinging to the lower lip petals, which are covered in cone-shaped cells that help them to grip on, as the plant dutifully opens its mouth.

Just gazing at these beautiful blooms will bring joy and help you to stay in the moment as you watch the bees come and go. In addition, the flowers have a very low allergen rating, since the pollen is both sticky and hidden for most of the time, making snapdragons a great choice for sufferers of hay fever. The flowers are edible, too, and can be used to decorate cakes or cocktails, and they last a long time in a vase, so you can enjoy them indoors. Cutting the stems will simply encourage the plant to produce new flowers, too, extending the display throughout the summer.

Snapdragons are easy to grow from seed in spring, and you may find that these so-called half-hardy annuals are actually pretty tolerant of low temperatures and survive from year to year in a pot of free-draining compost, tucked into a sheltered spot near the house. Sowing seeds is also restful, so take the time to raise a few plants on a windowsill indoors, planting them out after the frosts in late spring.

Himalayan birch

BETULA UTILIS

Benefits
Autumn foliage colour; pollinator plant

Height & spread
18 x 9m (60 x 30ft); smaller cultivars are available

Our spirits can be dampened in winter as short days and inclement weather deprive us of sunlight, but plants such as the Himalayan birch that draw us outside can lift our mood.

Gloomy skies and long nights in winter can affect the body's internal clock, disrupting the production of serotonin, which regulates our appetite and mood, and the sleep hormone melatonin. However, being outside in the garden can make us feel happier, and plants with winter interest such as birches help inspire us to leave the house. The stems of the Himalayan birch are its main attraction and when stripped of foliage they stand out in startling silhouette. The species *Betula utilis* has peeling coppery pink stems, while the designers' favourite *Betula utilis* subsp. *jacquemontii* has pure white stems that gleam in low winter sun.

It is a medium-sized to large tree, growing up to 18m (60ft) in height, so opt for a more compact cultivar such as 'Trinity College', which reaches just 6m (20ft), if you have a small garden. All have green leaves that turn buttery yellow in autumn before they fall, and dangling catkins in spring that dance in the breeze, features that hold our interest and elevate our mood. The foliage also feeds moth caterpillars in spring, helping to increase the biodiversity in our gardens. The tree will grow in most soils and in full sun or part shade.

Benefits
Autumn foliage colour; fragrant leaves

Height & spread
12 x 8m (40 x 26ft); smaller cultivars are available

Candyfloss tree

CERCIDIPHYLLUM JAPONICUM

You may have never heard of the candyfloss tree, but once you see it – or rather smell it – in autumn, the fragrant foliage will lift your spirits and remain in your memory forever.

The candyfloss tree, or katsura tree as it's also known, is named after the unusual sugary scent that the heart-shaped foliage emits when it turns from green to yellow, orange and pink just before it falls. This special gift can stop us in our tracks and lift our mood by bringing back memories of the summertime confection that we loved as children.

The candyfloss tree is suitable for medium-sized gardens, but a more compact cultivar, 'Boyd's Dwarf', which grows to just 4m (13ft), is also available for those with smaller spaces. This tree prefers a neutral to acid soil, and a sheltered spot in sun or part shade.

Armand clematis

CLEMATIS ARMANDII

Benefits
Scented flowers; evergreen leaves

Height & spread
Up to 26 x 2.5m (26 x 8ft)

Clematis are all beautiful plants, but the early flowering species, *C. armandii*, has the edge in spring, when its clusters of white, scented flowers are guaranteed to lift the spirits at a time when much of the garden is still asleep.

The dark green, slim leaves of this clematis are evergreen, too, offering another source of colour to boost our mental wellbeing in early spring. Another benefit to allergy sufferers are the blooms' low levels of pollen, which are rated just 3 out of 10 on the Ogren Plant Allergy Scale (OPALS)™. This scale, developed by horticulturist Thomas Ogren, assigns a rating from 1 to 10 to each plant, based on its allergen level, with 1 the lowest and 10 the highest. Many insect-pollinated plants such as clematis have a low rating, while grasses and birch trees, for example, are wind pollinated and send clouds of pollen into the air, causing grief to those with allergies.

To grow this beautiful plant, you will need a structure such as a wired fence, large trellis or mature tree for its twinning tendrils to grasp. You could match it with an apple tree, the blossom of which also has a low OPALS rating, and spring flowers such as crocuses, daffodils and tulips. It also makes a great choice for decorating the boundary walls or fences of a town or city garden, where pollution can exacerbate the effects of allergens.

The stems of the Armand clematis can reach up to 8m (26ft), and although it can be trimmed after flowering, it looks best when given space to perform to its full potential. It also prefers free-draining soil, a sunny aspect and some shelter from cold winds.

You may find that the leaves die off and fall during long, hot summers, but the plant will soon recover – a couple of doses of high-potassium fertilizer in late spring and early summer, given at fortnightly intervals, will encourage new growth.

Saffron

CROCUS SATIVUS

Benefits
Pollinator plant; edible flowers

Height & spread
30 x 15cm (12 x 6in)

Cooks will know that saffron is one of the world's most expensive spices, but gardeners may also be aware that the plant from which it is derived is actually very easy to grow.

The diminutive *Crocus sativu*s is an autumn-flowering bulb, and produces mauve goblet-shaped blooms, similar to those of its spring-flowering cousin, with bright red stigmas nestled inside, which are harvested and dried to make saffron. The flowers are surrounded by slim, grasslike green foliage.

The pretty blooms and saffron's delicate colour and taste make us happy, of course, but research also shows that compounds in the spice may act as a mild natural antidepressant, improving our mood. The nectar-rich flowers also attract bees, so perhaps grow enough for your needs and those of the garden wildlife, too.

If you want to grow and harvest your own saffron, buy bulbs from specialist suppliers and plant them in late summer or early autumn in a sunny spot and free-draining soil. Take care when ordering that you buy *Crocus sativus* and not the highly poisonous *Colchicum*, which is also known as autumn crocus or autumn saffron.

When the flowers bloom, use a pair of tweezers to remove the long floppy stigmas (bright red saffron threads) from each flower, avoiding the pale orange, upright stamens that carry the pollen. Leave the saffron threads to dry and store in an airtight container. Before use, you will need to rehydrate the threads in a few tablespoons of warm water for a few hours. For a pinch of saffron, you will need about 20 threads.

These crocus plants are hardy and will die down in the spring but reappear the following autumn, offering a harvest of saffron each year.

Maidenhair tree

GINKGO BILOBA

Benefits
Decorative leaves; autumn foliage colour

Height & spread
Up to 12 x 5m (40 x 16ft)

Often referred to as a "living fossil", the maidenhair tree is one of the oldest living tree species and provided food for plant-eating dinosaurs hundreds of millions of years ago. Today, its beauty and ancient heritage evoke feelings of strength and hope.

The tree is celebrated for its resilience and endurance, and specimens even survived the atomic bombing of Hiroshima in 1945, starting to bud soon afterwards. Showing little sign of long-term damage, they continue to thrive today, and the seeds of the atomic bomb survivors have been planted at gardens and arboretums around the world as symbols of peace and hope.

The oldest living maidenhair tree is thought to be 3,500 years of age, and in Asian countries it is often planted close to temples as a sign of enduring life.

In addition, *Ginkgo biloba* is known for its potential to improve memory and blood circulation, although the results from scientific studies are mixed on its levels of effectiveness.

From an aesthetic point of view, this beautiful native of China has many benefits. Adorned with textured brown stems and distinctive fan-shaped green leaves that sparkle in autumn when they turn a glittering shade of gold, it creates an uplifting feature in the garden. However, it grows into a large tree, and the smaller cultivar 'Mariken', which reaches just 2m (6ft 6in) in height, or the tiny 'Troll', are better choices for compact spaces.

While this tree is very resilient and will grow in most garden conditions, it favours full sun and a free-draining soil. The small cultivars can be grown in large pots of peat-free soil-based compost. It is also tolerant of pollution, which is why you may see it lining the streets of many towns and cities.

Just one note of caution: the seeds are toxic to pets, so choose a male plant that will not produce them.

Witch hazel

HAMAMELIS

Benefits
Scented flowers; autumn foliage colour

Height & spread
Ranging from 2.5–5m (8–16ft) in height and spread

Flowering just after the New Year's celebrations, when days are short and the landscape looks bleak, witch hazel comes to the rescue, lifting our spirits as winter deepens.

The unusual, spidery flowers of this large, deciduous shrub light up the garden, catching the eye with their scarlet, yellow or orange petals, although our noses often sense the sweet perfume first as it floats through the garden on frosty air. Smell is an emotive sense, with a unique ability to evoke memories, and if you enjoyed these winter flowers in childhood, the fragrance from new plants will transport you straight back to those innocent times.

As well as offering sparkling blooms with a delicious scent, tannins in the leaves and bark of this plant have an anti-inflammatory effect and topical preparations are used to treat a variety of conditions, including skin irritation, varicose veins and haemorrhoids, bringing welcome relief to those suffering with these ailments.

While the orange and red cultivars make a great visual impact, if it's scent you are looking for, choose a yellow-flowering variety. *Hamamelis* x *intermedia* 'Pallida' is one of the best, with a sweet fragrance reminiscent of freesias, while 'Arnold Promise' is another yellow cultivar with a sweet, heady scent. Or try 'Livia', which has red flowers and a light, spicy perfume. As days are short, bring a few stems indoors to enjoy them during the long winter evenings.

To grow one of these beautiful plants, you will need a sunny or lightly shaded site, since the flowering buds require good light to develop. Any soil, apart from chalky, will be perfect, but they do require moisture around their roots, so ensure they are watered while establishing and apply a 5cm (2in) mulch (layer) of well-rotted garden compost or manure over the root ball (leaving a gap around the stems), to help prevent the soil drying out in summer.

Honeysuckle

LONICERA PERICLYMENUM

Benefits
Scented flowers; pollinator plant; wildlife plant (food for birds)

Height & spread
8 x 4m (26 x 13ft), although smaller cultivars are available

The common honeysuckle is a much-loved cottage garden plant, its twining stems used to frame doors or archways, where its sweet, irresistible scent brings a smile to the faces of all who pass beneath its boughs.

The species *Lonicera periclymenum* has the strongest fragrance, the scent wafting on the air on warm summer evenings, luring us to its clusters of tubular flowers, and attracting moths to its rich stores of nectar and pollen. Bees and other pollinators also visit the plant, and you may see elephant hawk-moth caterpillars feeding on the nectar before they metamorphize into the beautiful pink and olive-coloured adults. The red berries that follow the flowers in late summer and autumn are also loved by birds and dormice.

Watching the wealth of wildlife this plant attracts helps to keep us mindful, restoring our tired brains and helping us to focus on work or other activities. The flowers' scent also helps to stimulate memories, perhaps of walks in the park or in the countryside, where you often see wild honeysuckle threaded through the hedgerows.

The flowers of the species are yellow and white, but there are also pink and red cultivars to choose from, including the late Dutch variety 'Serotina', which sports highly scented, deep red-purple flowers with yellow centres.

Honeysuckle is not a particularly fussy plant and will grow in most garden soils, bar waterlogged, and a site in full sun or part shade. It will need a framework for its twining stems to climb, so fix trellis or sturdy horizontal wires to a fence or wall, or let it scramble up a mature tree or through a wildlife hedge. Keep plants well-watered while their roots are establishing.

Forget-me-not

MYOSOTIS SYLVATICA

Benefits
Pollinator plant

Height & spread
30 x 20cm
(12 x 8in)

The forget-me-not brings cheer to gardens all over the world in spring when its clouds of tiny azure-blue flowers with yellow eyes appear, decorating every nook and cranny in the garden where the little seeds have fallen.

Symbolizing fond memories and lasting connections, the plant's name refers to its ability to self-seed, which means that once it finds a home in your garden, you'll never forget it, as the blue flowers pop up year after year. Unsurprisingly, it is also the flower of the Alzheimer's Society.

This little gem features in folklore, too, and it is associated with the story of a medieval knight who, while trying to pick the flowers beside a river for his beloved, fell into the water. Still clutching the posy, he called out "Forget me not" as he was swept away. For this reason, the flower is also associated with eternal love.

Forget-me-nots are loved by pollinators and provide much-needed early spring nectar and pollen for bees and butterflies.

For both new and more experienced gardeners alike, the forget-me-not is a gift that keeps on giving. It is very easy to grow: simply scatter the seeds on a bed, in a pot of peat-free compost, or in the cracks between paving, in full sun or part shade. This biennial will then produce stems of small, grey-green hairy leaves that overwinter, followed by clusters of tiny flowers the following spring. You can also buy cultivars in shades of pink and white, if you want to mix things up a little.

If you find it self-seeds too widely through the garden, simply pull up plants where they're not needed and remove the flowers before they scatter their seed.

NARCISSUS

Benefits
Scented flowers

Height & spread
Up to 60 x 20cm (24 x 10in); dwarf varieties are also available

Toxicity
Bulbs and flowers are toxic

Loved by poets and gardeners alike, the daffodil is one of the first flowers to show its face in early spring, with heads of cheerful yellow blooms welcoming in the new season.

It's impossible not to be charmed by this beautiful bulb, which has earned its place as the national flower of Wales, and a symbol of good luck and prosperity in China, where plants are forced into bloom to coincide with the country's New Year celebrations.

Yellow is a positive colour, too, and in studies many people associate it with joy and happiness. This bright, saturated hue is also stimulating and gives us energy, while blues and greens are more calming. Some daffodils are scented, which lifts our mood, and a few have white flowers.

The flower's namesake in Greek mythology is associated with themes of self-love, obsession and the consequences of vanity. In the legend, the beautiful Narcissus is cursed to fall in love with his reflection and, unable to tear himself away from his own image, he eventually wastes away and transforms into a daffodil. While this may not be the happiest of tales, the flower itself references Narcissus' beauty and symbolizes new beginnings and rebirth.

While the daffodil is poisonous to eat, it is being used in modern medicine, where an alkaloid called galantamine extracted from the plant helps to ease symptoms of cognitive decline in people with early-stage Alzheimer's disease.

Plant daffodil bulbs in autumn in pots of peat-free compost or in the ground for a colourful display the following year. The bulbs are inexpensive, so treat yourself to a range of different types to provide a continuous display from late winter to late spring. Plant them at three times the depth of the bulb, so if they measure 2.5cm (1in) from tip to base, plant them 7.5cm (3in) deep. The flowers prefer a moist but well-drained soil, but are not too fussy, and a location in full sun or part shade.

Benefits
Winter flowers; pollinator plant

Height & spread
4 x 4m (13 x 13 ft)

Winter-flowering cherry

PRUNUS × SUBHIRTELLA 'AUTUMNALIS'

For many, winter's long, dark nights and icy conditions can make us feel a little gloomy, but nature is always on hand to provide an antidote to the weather and bring us cheer.

The dainty white blooms of the winter-flowering cherry offer medicine for the soul, dusting the tree's bare branches like snowflakes from late autumn to early spring. For those who wish to add some colour, try the cultivar 'Autumnalis Rosea', with its semi-double pale pink flowers.

This is a tree that keeps on giving, and after a quiet period in summer when the green leaves unfurl, offering welcome shade, the foliage lights up the garden in autumn with fiery reds, yellows and oranges before falling.

The winter-flowering cherry will reward you with plenty of blooms when planted in a sunny spot and any soil, as long as it isn't waterlogged.

Lamb's ears

STACHYS BYZANTINA

Benefits
Tactile foliage; pollinator plant

Height & spread
20 x 45cm
(8 x 18in)

The soft, furry leaves of lamb's ears give rise to this plant's name and just call out to be touched. Children in particular find the foliage intriguing, its downy texture similar to a cuddly teddy bear.

The silvery colour is also attractive, shimmering in the sunshine, while in summer, the velvety stems are studded with small pink flowers that attract pollinators such as bees.

The tactile nature of this pretty evergreen perennial makes us feel good, but it is also a tough, resilient little plant that will sail through months of drought unharmed. Its armour against strong sun and dry soil is the silver colour which reflects light and the fine hairs that trap dew and moisture. As it is adapted to thrive in these arid conditions, plant it in full sun and free-draining soil – it will sulk in shade and damp clay. When happy, it will spread of its own accord to fill the front of a border.

French marigold

TAGETES PATULA

Benefits
Scented flowers; pollinator plant (single-flowered varieties); edible flowers

Height & spread
Up to 45 x 45cm (18 x 18in); shorter varieties are available

These joyful little plants with their sunny orange and yellow flowers are a mainstay of cottage-style gardens, blooming continuously from early summer to the first frosts in autumn.

While Europeans have been enjoying marigolds for hundreds of years, they are, in fact, natives of Mexico and Guatemala, and were brought back by plant hunters and cultivated by the French, in particular, who loved the flowers' bright colours and their scent, which is used in the perfume industry.

In Mexico, marigolds are used for Day of the Dead, or Día de los Muertos, to symbolize the beauty and fragility of life and the joy of reunion with ancestors, even in death. The flowers are believed to bring happiness to the souls of the departed on the day of the festival, when they temporarily return to Earth.

Other cultures have also embraced the little plants. Bright orange and yellow marigold flowers are used to make garlands and dress altars to bring light and positivity, and to honour ancestors, in the Hindu festival of Diwali.

The flowers are edible, too, and can be used to add colourful garnishes to salads, soups, desserts and cocktails. They are also used in herbal remedies to soothe indigestion, colic, constipation and dysentery, although their effectiveness is not scientifically proven.

Bees and other pollinators love the single-flowered types (those with daisy-like flowers), which offer rich stores of nectar and pollen, and watching these creatures dance from plant to plant can be restorative and help us to relax.

The plants are not frost hardy, but they can be grown from seed on a windowsill indoors in spring and planted out later in the season, or you can buy small plug plants to grow on. They like sun and a free-draining soil, or plant a few in a pot of peat-free compost to decorate a terrace or balcony.

TRIFOLIUM

Benefits
Pollinator plant (single-flowered varieties); edible flowers and leaves

Height & spread
Up to 10 x 10cm (4 x 4in)

This humble, diminutive plant that grows among the grasses in our lawns has long been associated with good luck and happiness.

The most common clover is the white species, *Trifolium repens*, which usually has three leaves, but occasionally one may produce four and it is these anomalies that are said to bring good luck.

The plant is also a symbol of Ireland and known there as shamrock – Saint Patrick, one of the country's patron saints, used it as a metaphor for the Christian Holy Trinity.

Clover is lucky for pollinators, too, since its flowers are rich sources of nectar and pollen. It's also a legume and, as such, it hosts bacteria that fix the plant nutrient nitrogen from the air in nodules in its roots. Nitrogen is the most abundant gas in the Earth's atmosphere, so clovers have an infinite supply, whereas other plants must source it from the ground, where it can become depleted. Clover is also lucky for the grasses in which it grows because when it dies it releases nitrogen into the soil to feed them and keep the lawn green.

Pansy

VIOLA

Benefits
Edible flowers and leaves

Height & spread
15 x 15cm (6 x 6in)

Everyone loves a pansy, their little round faces and whiskery markings raising a smile, especially in winter, when few other plants are in flower.

The wild pansy, *Viola tricolor*, will pop up in the garden from self-sown seed and has a variety of common names, including heart's ease and come-and-cuddle-me, referencing its link to love and romance. It generally has dark purple and white flowers with yellow eyes, while cultivars come in a huge assortment of shades to suit all tastes, and you can choose from dainty violas to the larger-flowered pansies. The flowers are also edible and help to brighten up salads and decorate cakes.

Pansies and violas are easy to grow, and ideal for pots on a patio or balcony or a windowbox, where you can see them up close. Plant in peat-free potting compost and keep them well-watered, but guard against waterlogging, which could rot them – pots with drainage holes at the bottom are essential for them to thrive.

Soothing the senses

The colours and scents of many plants can help us to relax and calm frayed nerves, while the shape of some flowers holds our attention, allowing the brain to switch off and recharge.

BELLIS PERENNIS

Benefits
Pollinator plant; wildlife plant (food for birds); calming flowers; edible flowers and leaves

Height & spread
Up to 10 x 10cm (4 x 4in)

One of the first flowers that children can recognize and name, the daisy is a happy plant, drawing us to its bountiful blooms, with their delicate white petals and bright yellow eyes.

Daisies can also help us to relax because of the flowers' repetitive patterns, known as fractals, which hold our attention, take our minds off other worries, and help us to recover from stress. Fractals occur frequently in nature and landscapes, but research shows that we are particularly attracted to daisy, buttercup and lily flowers with a radially symmetrical pattern because it is easy for our brains to process.

Daisies have other benefits, too, and have long been used in herbal preparations to help heal wounds. Research has shown that the flowers contain saponins, which are found in collagen, a building block of the skin, suggesting that these traditional daisy-based remedies do, in fact, have healing properties.

Aside from the science, daisies are fun. Making daisy chains with children is relaxing and helps them to form a bond with nature and memories they will cherish as they grow. The simple joy this little plant brings has given rise to it symbolizing new beginnings, innocence and happiness in many cultures.

For wildlife, the daisy can be a lifesaver, its flowers opening in early spring to sustain bees, moths and other pollinators with nectar and pollen, while the seeds nourish many birds. The plant's spoon-shaped evergreen foliage also provides shelter for insects and other beneficial organisms, and both the leaves and flowers are edible and can be added to salads or used as garnishes.

You don't need to cultivate daisies, they will appear of their own accord, but do refrain from using weedkillers on lawns and in the garden, which not only kill these beautiful plants but adversely affect the environment.

Chocolate cosmos

COSMOS ATROSANGUINEUS

Benefits
Scented flowers

Height & spread
60 x 45cm
(24 x 18in)

For chocolate lovers who find themselves drawn to the scent of cocoa, this is the plant for you, its dark red flowers emitting the tantalizing fragrance of this delicious confection.

The chocolate cosmos has been a favourite cottage garden plant in the UK ever since it was introduced from Mexico over a century ago. It helps to soothe the senses with its wonderful aroma, the source of which is an organic compound called vanillin, found in both the flowers and in cacao beans, which are used to make chocolate.

Chocolate itself is associated with love and happiness, and for good reason. It contains the amino acid tryptophan that's needed in the production of serotonin, a neurotransmitter which enhances mood, making us feel happy and content. Smell is a powerful sense, too, and just a whiff of chocolate is associated with the taste of this delicious sweet treat. However, despite their smell, these flowers are not edible.

This perennial is easy to grow: buy young plants in spring and plant in full sun and free-draining soil in garden borders or containers filled with peat-free multipurpose compost. Try cultivars with the strongest scent, such as 'Chocamocha' or 'Cherry Chocolate', a compact variety that's a little hardier than the species and sports cherry-red flowers, still with the same fragrance. To enjoy the aroma of your plants all summer, remove the faded blooms promptly, which will extend the show.

Unlike the common *Cosmos bipinnatus*, which is an annual plant, this perennial will flower from year to year, but it is not completely hardy, so to guarantee its survival, set plants in a sheltered spot over winter, or take cuttings and keep them on a windowsill indoors until the following late spring.

Hawthorn

CRATAEGUS MONOGYNA

Benefits
Autumn berries; pollinator plant; wildlife plant (food for birds)

Height & spread
Up to 4 x 4m (13 x 13ft)

Also known as the May thorn, this hedgerow tree or shrub has been used in pagan May Day festivals for centuries as a symbol of the new season, its spiny stems of white or pink blooms woven into garlands and wreaths.

Hawthorn's spring flowers are a magnet for bees and butterflies, and the berries that follow in late summer and autumn are loved by birds. The thorny stems provide birds with safe nesting and roosting sites, too, and studies show that the activities of wildlife in the garden help to hold our focus, allowing our brains to relax and reboot.

Meanwhile, birdsong has a restorative effect on us, so any plant that draws in small birds with tuneful voices has a positive impact on our health. Some experts believe that human language and birdsong evolved at the same time, which may explain our appreciation of this natural music. Others think it is because we associate birdsong with happy memories of being in a garden or walks in the countryside on warm spring and summer days, when birds are most vocal.

Hawthorn berries have been used in folk medicine as a remedy for heart disease, and more recent studies show that they contain antioxidants, including oligomeric procyanidins (OPCs) that may help dilate blood vessels, improving blood flow and helping to improve circulatory problems. In *Grow Your Own Drugs*, James Wong suggests they may also help with Raynaud's disease. Like many red and purple fruits, hawthorn berries are sources of quercetin, too, which is an antioxidant that may reduce inflammation.

While the flesh of the berries is edible, always seek advice from your doctor before eating large quantities, especially if you have a heart condition or are taking other medications. The seeds are toxic and not for consumption.

You can buy inexpensive bare-root hawthorn plants in winter to make a hedge or plant a solitary tree. The trees develop beautiful twining trunks and branches that add to their charm. Plant hawthorn in a sunny or partly shaded spot in any reasonable garden soil, bar waterlogged.

Globe thistle

ECHINOPS

Benefits
Relaxing blue flowers; pollinator plant; wildlife plant (food for birds)

Height & spread
1.2m x 45cm (4ft x 18in)

A cottage garden favourite, the globe thistle is a tall plant decked with thistle-like spiny dark green leaves and spherical blue flowerheads held aloft on sturdy stems throughout summer.

The flowers are adored by bees, butterflies and other pollinators, and the seeds that follow are loved by birds, bringing a theatrical spectacle of wildlife to the garden through the summer and autumn. The restorative effect of watching the insects and birds toing and froing is relaxing (see also hawthorn, pp.42–3), while the gentle hum of bees and the twittering of small birds is known to reduce stress.

In addition, the symmetrical pattern of the globe thistle's flowerheads is calming, and recent research into the colour blue showed that it, too, helps to lower stress levels. Blue is the favourite colour of many people, perhaps reminding us of the ocean, lakes and a clear sky, and in studies babies gazed at the colour for longer than other hues. While blue is often associated in popular culture with sadness, it seems that it has the oppositive effect on our moods. In Japan, after blue lights were installed at 71 Japanese train stations, the suicide rate decreased by an amazing 84 per cent, while crime rates fell when blue lights were installed in Glasgow.

To grow this calming, hardy perennial plant, all you need is a sunny or partly shaded site and free-draining soil. It will then deliver its pretty flowering stems every year, dying down in winter and emerging again the following spring.

Common hop

HUMULUS LUPULUS

Benefits
Relaxing summer flowers; autumn foliage colour

Height & spread
Up to 16 x 6m (20 x 20ft)

Many people will know hops as an ingredient in beer, adding to the flavour and helping to preserve its frothy head, but fewer may be aware that the flowers of this climbing perennial can also help to reduce anxiety and promote a good night's sleep.

A large, deciduous climber, hop features ornamental lobed leaves that turn bright yellow in autumn, and in summer cone-like flowerheads on female plants hang from the vine like tiny bunches of grapes. To help you rest and relax, remove stems of flowers and hang them upside down in a well-ventilated place indoors to dry before popping them into a muslin bag. Place the bag in your pillowcase, where the compounds and essential oils in the flowers will help you to sleep.

While the species is generally only used in commercial cultivation, the beautiful golden hop, *Humulus lupulus* 'Aureus', is a valued garden climber. Plant it next to a wired wall or fence or a large section of trellis, or allow it to scramble over a wired pergola. It needs a sunny or lightly shaded site and free-draining soil to thrive. This climber dies back in winter.

Busy lizzie

IMPATIENS WALLERIANA

Benefits
Colourful flowers; fascinating seed heads

Height & spread
15 x 20cm (6 x 8in)

Loved for its round, long-lasting flowers, which come in a wide range of beautiful jewel-like shades, the busy lizzie has long been a staple of summer gardens in Europe and America.

The plant's ability to flower in shade, where few brightly coloured plants are happy, is part of the allure, and while the scarlet and fuchsia pink varieties are hardly restful, it performs a little trick that helps our brains to pause for a moment, and become distracted from stresses and worries.

The Latin name *Impatiens*, meaning "impatient", is a clue. As the seed heads ripen, they burst open when touched, exploding with an impatience to disperse their cargo far and wide. This can be fascinating for the onlooker, helping us to stay in the moment and offering time for the brain to rest.

These tender African perennials are grown in cool climates each year as annuals. Plant them after the frosts in late spring in a sunny or shaded site, in pots of peat-free compost or in moist but free-draining soil in the garden.

Jasmine

JASMINUM

Benefits
Soothing scented flowers; pollinator plant

Height & spread
Up to 4 x 1.5m (13 x 5ft)

Known as the Queen of Flowers, jasmine or yasmin means "a gift from God" in Persian, and this climbing beauty certainly lives up to its name, with twining stems of small green leaves and white, highly scented flowers.

Jasmine's summer and early autumn blooms have many attributes and research studies show that the oil derived from them can help to reduce insomnia, palpitations and irritability, while generally helping to soothe frayed nerves. Other studies show the plant can improve memory, mental accuracy and visual awareness. The oil also has an antibacterial effect and can be used to fight various bacteria when applied to the skin.

The flowers' scent alone makes this a happy plant, too. The foundation of the perfume industry, jasmine is known simply as *La Fleur*, or "The Flower", reflecting its importance. For those of us growing it in our gardens, the scent floating on a summer breeze may bring memories of a loved one, perhaps someone who wore perfume based on its scent, and of halcyon days with family and friends.

The fragrance is most powerful in the evening, luring night-flying insects such as moths. The flower's structure is specially adapted to those with long tongues, including hawk moths, which can reach inside to harvest the nectar.

There are many species of jasmine to choose from, the hardiest of which is the common jasmine (*Jasminum officinale*), or try the large-flowered *Jasminum grandiflorum* against a warm, sunny wall. Tender types include the perfumier's favourites *J. sambac* and *J. polyanthum*, which can be grown in a conservatory or heated greenhouse. All varieties will require a framework to climb, so either install wires on a wall or fence, or grow it up a large trellis. To thrive, jasmine prefers a sunny site and free-draining soil; prune out old shoots after flowering to keep it within bounds.

Lavender

LAVANDULA

Benefits
Soothing scented flowers; pollinator plant; edible flowers

Height & spread
Up to 1 x 1m (39 x 39in)

Lavender is a staple of romantic cottage gardens, while the power of its flowers to soothe the senses has been known for centuries, and it is still used today to promote a good night's sleep.

This aromatic herb has always been revered, and it was even found in the tomb of Tutankhamun in Egypt, where its fragrance could still be detected when it was discovered thousands of years later in 1922. Recent research confirms that the flowers help us to relax and placing a posy in a pillow is a safe remedy for people suffering with mild insomnia.

The RHS's own research also shows that people link the scent to feeling calm and happy, while other studies have found that essential oils made from lavender help to decrease anxiety and stress, and increase feelings of contentment. However, take care, as the oil can irritate sensitive skins and women should consult their doctors before using it if they are pregnant or breastfeeding.

The purple-blue colour may also influence our positive response to the plant, since it, too, is thought to help us unwind (see also p.44). Wildlife is drawn to the colour and fragrance of lavender flowers, and plants are covered in bees and butterflies when they bloom in summer. Watching the comings and goings of these pollinators is restorative, helping the mind to switch off when focusing on their activities, and allowing us to return to our tasks feeling refreshed. The flowers are also edible and can be used as garnishes and to flavour cakes and drinks.

One of the most aromatic species is English lavender (*Lavandula angustifolia*), which was first introduced to Britain from the Mediterranean region by the Romans. An evergreen shrub with grey-green leaves and spikes of purple flowers, it needs full sun and a well-drained soil to thrive. Grow it as a low hedge or dot the shrubs around the garden; alternatively, plant it in pots if you have heavy clay or soil prone to waterlogging.

Lavandula × *intermedia* is another good option for scent and a long flowering season. It requires the same conditions as English lavender to thrive.

Lemon balm

MELISSA OFFICINALIS

Benefits
Scented foliage; pollinator plant; calming edible flowers and leaves

Height & spread
Up to 1 x 1m (39 x 39in)

The mild lemon flavour of this tall perennial herb has been used to make calming teas for hundreds of years, while the effects of traditional lemon balm remedies to improve memory, and reduce anxiety, irritability and insomnia, have been upheld by modern science.

This aromatic herb has also been approved in Germany for the treatment of flatulence and digestive tract spasms, while scientific research is ongoing into the plant's antiviral and antibacterial properties.

Lemon balm is a magnet for pollinators, which are attracted to the nectar-laden spikes of creamy white or pale purple flowers that appear in summer. The scent of the heart-shaped leaves also lures honeybees – its botanical name *Melissa* means 'honeybee' in Greek. The foliage contains many of the same chemicals that are found in bee pheromones, and beekeepers use the crushed foliage to coax worker bees to take up home in new hives.

To enjoy the benefits of this herb, simply grow it in your garden in full sun or part shade and free-draining soil, or in a large container of peat-free potting compost on a balcony or terrace. Plants tend to spread rapidly and are best confined to large pots to prevent them overwhelming their neighbours in a border. Growing it in a container on a patio by the back door allows you to harvest the leafy stems easily to flavour salads, sauces and fish dishes, or to make herbal tea.

You can also infuse a few handfuls of leaves in a pan of boiling water for 10–15 minutes, leave it to cool, and then pour into a bath for a relaxing soak in the lemony water.

Benefits
Fascinating foliage

Height & spread
Up to 30 x 25cm
(12 x 10in)

Sensitive plant

MIMOSA PUDICA

Known as the sensitive or tickle-me plant, this tender perennial has fascinating leaves that fold up when touched, and then gradually recover and unfurl after a few hours.

This plant's little trick is intriguing and keeps us focused, allowing us to be mindful for a moment or two and helping the brain to relax and reboot (see also p.50).

The folding response is triggered by touch. When the leaves detect physical pressure, specialized cells called mechanoreceptors are triggered, which cause the plant to lose water through the cells and the leaves then droop. The ferny foliage is accompanied in summer by fluffy pale pink or pale purple pom-pom flowers that add to the show.

Buy young plants in late spring or sow seed earlier in the season on a warm windowsill indoors, planting it out after the frosts in full sun or part shade and a moist but free-draining soil, or in pots of peat-free compost. Bring it indoors before the frosts in autumn.

Benefits
Rustling foliage; decorative flowers and seed heads

Height & spread
2.2 x 1.5m (7 x 5 ft); smaller varieties are also available

Plants that engage our senses help us to stay focused in the moment, or mindful, which research says helps to improve our mental wellbeing. Colour and scent top the agenda, but sound can also help to soothe frayed nerves.

Planting grasses such as *Miscanthus* that rustle in the breeze is calming due to the gentle, repetitive sound they create. Like the rippling of water, this natural melody helps us to relax and enjoy a sense of peace, reducing stress levels. Other grasses that offer a soothing soundscape include switch grass (*Panicum*) and feather reed grass (*Calamagrostis*).

Miscanthus is a tall, elegant, deciduous grass with green linear leaves – some cultivars also sport a silvery white or reddish-tinged midrib – which turn brown over winter, while plumes of silvery to pale pink flowers appear in late summer and autumn. Grow it in any reasonable garden soil, and cut the brown foliage and flower stems down at the end of winter.

Eulalia

MISCANTHUS SINENSIS

Water lily

NYMPHAEA

Benefits
Attractive foliage and flowers; wildlife plant (habitat for aquatic creatures)

Spread
Up to 3m (10ft) or more, depending on the cultivar

An afternoon relaxing beside a reflective pool or patio water feature dotted with water lilies is one of life's simple pleasures, where the cares of the day simply evaporate away.

We have all experienced this positive feeling, so it will come as no surprise to discover that research studies have found people living near water are healthier and happier than the rest of the population. The elixir of life, water can help to reduce stress and makes us feel restored and rejuvenated. Still water also reflects light, clouds and blue sky into the garden, and gazing at this slow-moving scene helps us to relax.

Water lilies provide the icing on the cake, their symmetrical shape holding our attention and helping our brains to switch off (see also p.50). Try gazing at these flowers for a few minutes after performing a challenging task or a stressful day to feel their restorative effect.

In Asian cultures the lilies symbolize rebirth and resurrection, a reference to the way the petals close up at night and open again at dawn, although some are night-bloomers and open in the evening and close during the day.

The plants also play host to a range of wildlife, including frogs, toads and all manner of aquatic insects. The leaves and flowers shade the pond surface, reducing the growth of algae, while the roots help to absorb excess nutrients from fertilizers and decaying vegetation that can find their way into water and cause pollution.

Choose a dwarf water lily, such as *Nymphaea* 'Pygmaea Helvola', for a small pool or opt for a cultivar such as the pink 'Escarboucle' or pale lemon 'Marliacea Chromatella' to fill a larger pond. Before buying, check your chosen plant's preferred water depth – the roots and stems should be submerged to that depth, while the leaves float on the surface. Plant in a pond basket filled with aquatic compost and place it on bricks if the water is too deep.

Passion flower

PASSIFLORA

Benefits
Fascinating flowers; edible fruits (of some species)

Height & spread
Up to 10 x 2m (30ft x 6ft 6in)

The intricate patterns of a passion flower's summer blooms lure you in to take a closer look, helping to keep the brain focused and mindful.

Research into the edible apricot vine (*Passiflora incarnata*) also shows that it increases gamma-aminobutyric acid (GABA) in the brain, which helps us feel more relaxed, and reduces the symptoms of insomnia, anxiety and depression, while further studies are exploring the medicinal uses of the plant.

The name of this climbing deciduous vine refers to the passion of Jesus – Spanish Christian missionaries used the unique structures of the blooms as symbols to represent Christ at his crucifixion.

The delicious egg-shaped yellow or purple fruits are harvested from the species *Passiflora edulis*, and the flesh is used to flavour drinks, cakes and desserts. They are rich in vitamins and fibre, and may offer a range of health benefits, including managing inflammatory and neurological diseases, and helping to reduce high blood pressure and protect against heart disease.

However, the fruits of the more widely grown blue passion flower (*Passiflora caerulea*) are bitter and edible only when fully ripe – unripe fruit and the leaves contain cyanogenic glycosides, which turn into cyanide when eaten, although they are both so bitter that you wouldn't be tempted to consume them.

The species *Passiflora incarnata* is not widely available to buy, but you will find the tender *Passiflora edulis* for sale and can enjoy the fruits if you have a conservatory or heated greenhouse to protect it over winter. Or, in mild areas, plant it in a large pot of peat-free compost, train it up a sunny, south-facing wall in summer, and cover it with fleece in winter. The hardier *Passiflora caerulea* also needs a sunny spot and well-drained soil to thrive, but should sail through winters unaided in sheltered gardens. These vines all need a sturdy support, such as trellis or horizontal wires, for the stems to climb.

Scots pine

PINUS SYLVESTRIS

Benefits
Decorative bark and cones; calming leaves and shoots; edible nuts

Height & spread
Up to 25 x 10m (80 x 30ft)

Tall and stately, this beautiful pine is Scotland's national tree and known as the King of the Scottish woods due to its height, the durability of its wood, and the distinctive orange textured bark, blue-green needles and decorative cones.

The Scots pine has many health benefits, too, and it is included here because herbal teas made from the young shoots and needles have a calming effect, reducing stress by supporting the adrenal glands – the leaves are also rich in vitamin C. Studies show that it can help to improve focus and restore energy in those suffering with depression, too.

Research by the Japanese scientist Dr Qing Li, who invented the idea of "forest bathing", found that trees emit airborne chemicals called phytoncides, which have an anti-inflammatory effect, strengthen our immune system and help to reduce stress and anxiety. He also discovered that conifers, especially pines and cypresses, produce higher levels of these chemicals than most deciduous trees (oaks being the one exception).

The resin and needles of the pine can treat some respiratory problems, too, and placing a muslin bag containing the needles in your pillowcase may help to relieve catarrh. The edible nuts, which can be harvested from the cones, have a similar effect and may protect against heart disease by reducing "bad" cholesterol.

This pine is only suitable for a large garden, as it can grow to a towering 25m (80ft) or more, although the canopy is relatively compact, so it won't cast too much shade. It enjoys full sun and well-drained, sandy soil. In smaller gardens, replicate the image of this majestic tree with the shorter *Pinus sylvestris* 'Watereri' (pictured), which reaches a maximum height of 3–6m (10–20ft). For the beneficial effects of forest bathing in a small courtyard garden, you could try the hinoki cypress *Chamaecyparis obtusa* 'Torulosa Dwarf', which grows to just over a metre (3ft) and can be planted in a large container of loam-based compost.

Damask rose

ROSA × DAMASCENA

Benefits
Soothing scented flowers

Height & spread
1.5 x 1.2m (5 x 4ft)

Symbolizing romance, love, beauty and courage, the rose has long been regarded as variously the king or queen of flowers, its exquisite blooms and alluring fragrance adorning gardens for thousands of years.

This old-fashioned rose, named after the city of Damascus in modern-day Syria, is thought to have been brought to Northern Europe by the Romans or Crusaders, and the oil derived from it was used as a herbal remedy to relieve an assortment of conditions, from painful periods to chest pains. Modern scientific studies support many of the claims made about the rose, and show that when used in aromatherapy it helps us to relax and get a good night's sleep, soothes tired muscles, and acts as a mild antidepressant.

The fragrance from this highly scented old rose is one of the building blocks of the perfume industry, while the flowers can also bring back happy memories of loved ones who may have worn the fragrance, or summer days relaxing in the garden when the plants were in bloom (see also pp.48–9). The shape and intricate pattern of the flowers fascinates us, too, allowing the brain to take a break, unwind and recharge, before we move on to another task.

You will find damask roses in an assortment of colours, but all tend to flower just once in summer on prickly stems of disease-resistant green foliage. Roses enjoy a sunny position and moist but free-draining soil, although you will find that these old-fashioned types are quite forgiving and will also flower well in part shade.

Rosemary

SALVIA ROSMARINUS

Benefits
Soothing scented foliage; scented flowers; pollinator plant

Height & spread
1.5 x 1.5m (5 x 5ft)

This common, evergreen, shrubby herb, grown primarily to flavour meat dishes, has long been used in traditional therapies to help improve memory, reduce anxiety and elevate our mood.

Dubbed a "wonder herb", rosemary has been associated with memory for hundreds of years. Shakespeare was aware of this power, and in *Hamlet*, Ophelia declares, "There's rosemary, that's for remembrance. Pray you, love, remember!" The quote may also reference the herb's use at weddings, when Elizabethan brides carried it to symbolize happiness, loyalty and love.

There have been a few compelling research studies into rosemary's ability to heighten alertness and concentration, and reduce anxiety. In 2015, a study of 60 older volunteers found that inhaling the aroma of rosemary oil helped improve their memory, while another showed that it significantly increased the alertness of young school children. Research by scientists at Nottingham University also found that pupils exposed to the scent of rosemary essential oil achieved 5–7 per cent better results than a control group in memory tests.

In traditional therapies, the herb is used to treat a number of other conditions. Rosemary has antibacterial and antifungal properties, and European herbal remedies include it in ointments to help heal wounds and soothe eczema. A tea made by infusing the leaves and flowers in boiling water for five to ten minutes is thought to relieve headaches, colic and depression.

This hardy shrub has dark green, needle-like, evergreen foliage and small blue flowers in spring. Grow it in the garden and benefit from its healing powers by adding sprigs to your savoury dishes and make teas by infusing the foliage in boiling water. Ideally, plant it in a sheltered, sunny site, although it will cope with part shade, and free-draining soil. Alternatively, grow it in a large pot of peat-free soil-based compost, with some handfuls of grit for extra drainage.

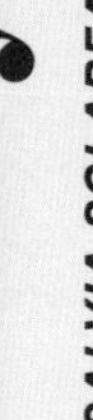

SALVIA SCLAREA

Benefits
Soothing scented foliage; pollinator plant

Height & spread
90 x 40cm (36 x 16in)

A relative of the culinary herb sage, clary sage will decorate your garden with its highly scented, wrinkled, oblong leaves and spikes of long-lasting pale pink hooded flowers with mauve bracts.

Clary sage has hidden qualities that set it apart from other perennials in the garden, and it has been used for thousands of years in traditional remedies to treat a range of conditions, including inflammation, pain and menstrual cramps. Recent research confirms that the essential oil extracted from the herb and used in aromatherapy contains sclareol, which has an anti-inflammatory effect and helps soothe uterine pain, while other studies show that the plant may help to relieve depression caused by the menopause.

The distilled essential oil is used widely in perfumes, too, and as a muscatel-like flavouring for vermouths, wines, liqueurs and beer.

The herb helps to soothe the senses in other ways when it blooms, as the colourful flowers attract a host of pollinators that capture our imagination and help our brains to relax and reboot (see p.50).

To grow this short-lived Mediterranean perennial, sow the seeds in spring on a windowsill indoors or in a heated greenhouse. Transplant the seedlings into individual pots when they have a few sets of leaves and grow on indoors until all risk of frost has passed in late spring. You can then transplant them into the garden in moist but well-drained soil and full sun or light, partial shade. Alternatively, grow them in patio pots in peat-free multipurpose potting compost, and water well during dry spells.

Rowan

SORBUS AUCUPARIA

Benefits
Autumn foliage colour; pollinator plant; wildlife plant (food for birds); edible berries

Height & spread
Up to 8 x 6m (26 x 20ft)

Known as rowan or mountain ash, this European native has many attributes that soothe the senses and reduce stress, its leafy canopy helping to lower levels of inflammation, a key factor in heart disease, cancer and diabetes.

Research shows that urban trees such as rowans improve our wellbeing, with people living in areas with new tree cover showing significantly lower levels of inflammation, which is known to be a contributor to many medical conditions, including cancer.

In terms of their calming effects, rowans are particularly beneficial because they offer many wildlife benefits that influence our mood. The pollen-rich white spring blossom attracts pollinators, while the orange-red autumn berries are loved by birds, and studies show that watching wildlife is restorative and helps us to relax, while birdsong also brings us a sense of peace (see pp.42–43). In addition, the shade afforded by trees offers a relaxing retreat on hot summer's days, and the bright red or yellow autumn foliage lights up the garden as the nights draw in.

Rowan berries are edible and rich in vitamins, especially vitamins C and E and provitamin A, as well as minerals such as iron, copper, zinc, potassium and magnesium. The fruits have been used in traditional therapies for centuries to treat gastrointestinal problems, and are believed to help ward off infections by bolstering the immune system. The sweetest berries are from *Sorbus aucuparia* var. *edulis*, but eat them sparingly, as they contain parasorbic acid, which can lead to kidney damage or other gastrointestinal problems if consumed in large quantities. Also consult your doctor before eating rowan berries if you are pregnant, breastfeeding or taking other medications.

This deciduous tree is very hardy and suitable for gardens in urban areas, where it shrugs off atmospheric pollution. However, it can grow into a large tree, so for smaller spaces, try the cultivar 'Beissneri' or the conical-shaped 'Fastigiata'. Buy bare-root trees in the winter and plant in free-draining soil in a sunny or partly shaded area.

Benefits
Calming flowers; pollinator plant

Height & spread
12 x 8m (40 x 26ft); can be grown as a hedge

Lime tree

TILIA

The lime, or linden tree, with its heart-shaped leaves, fragrant pollen-rich summer flowers and autumn colour, provides a beautiful statement in medium-sized to large gardens.

As well as providing the raft of health benefits delivered by garden trees, tea made from the dried blossom flowers of the lime species *Tilia cordata* and *Tilia platyphyllos* has long been used in traditional folk medicine to reduce anxiety and promote better sleep. It is also used to treat colds, although there is little scientific evidence to prove its effectiveness in this regard.

The trees provide food for several moth species and attract aphids, which in turn lure ladybirds and birds that eat them. Limes are woodland trees and can grow into large specimens, so check that you have space for one before buying – *Tilia cordata* can be kept in check by using it as hedging. Plant in well-drained soil in full sun or part shade.

Benefits
Scented flowers; pollinator plant

Height & spread
150 x 60cm (5 x 2ft)

This perennial is a tall, billowing herb with airy sprays of small white scented flowers in summer, while the roots are used in traditional therapies to promote sleep and reduce anxiety.

Historically, valerian roots were also used to treat migraines and stomach cramps, but currently there is not enough scientific evidence to prove their effectiveness.

While valerian supplements are generally safe to take in the short term by most adults, consult your doctor first and do not use if you are pregnant or breastfeeding, or already taking medication for sleep or anxiety.

The plants themselves are beneficial, however, with the nectar-rich flowers bringing bees, butterflies, hoverflies and moths into the garden, which fascinate us and produce a calming effect.

To grow this tall herb, plant it in moist but free-draining soil in a sunny or partly shaded site. As a perennial, it will die down in winter, reappearing again the following spring.

Valerian

VALERIANA OFFICINALIS

Nature's food store

Research shows that the soothing hum of bees and flash of colourful butterfly wings lifts our spirits and these plants all attract a host of fascinating creatures, guaranteed to bring you joy and increase biodiversity.

Ornamental onion

ALLIUM

Benefits
Pollinator plant

Height & spread
Up to 1 x 0.5m (39 x 20in), although many are smaller

Easy to grow and offering an abundance of beautiful blooms that enrich the garden's biodiversity, alliums will make both you and the local wildlife very happy.

Ornamental alliums are related to edible onions, garlic, leeks and chives, and the flowers of all these species help to support a range of pollinators, including bees, butterflies, hoverflies and moths. The purple and violet blooms of many ornamental onions and the various insects that visit these flowers are both relaxing and fascinating, helping to keep our minds focused and rebooting the brain so that we can concentrate on new tasks (see also p.50).

These perennial bulbs come in an assortment of shapes and sizes to suit many garden situations. For small spaces, try either the compact American onion (*Allium unifolium*) with its grey-green leaves and star-shaped purple-pink, late spring flowers, or *Allium neapolitanum*, which bears sprays of dainty, white star-shaped blooms at the same time. The yellow-flowered *Allium moly* is also a short species, but as it spreads rapidly and could overwhelm a small garden, confine it to larger spaces such as meadows.

At the other extreme are the tall, pompon varieties, including the popular Dutch garlic, *Allium hollandicum* 'Purple Sensation', with its spherical heads of tiny, deep violet, star-shaped blooms, or the giant 'Globemaster', whose tall stems are topped with huge balls of violet-purple blooms in summer. If left uncut, the seed heads of later-flowering forms also provide habitats for overwintering insects – those that bloom in late spring generally lose their structure by autumn.

Plant the bulbs in early autumn in full sun or light, partial shade in free-draining soil, burying them at a depth of about twice the height of the bulb, with the flat section from which the roots will grow at the bottom.

Plume thistle

CIRSIUM RIVULARE

Benefits
Pollinator plant; wildlife plant (food for caterpillars and birds)

Height & spread
1.2 x 0.6m (4x 2ft)

The plume thistle is an elegant hardy perennial plant that produces tall, leafy stems topped with small, dark red thistle-like flowers throughout summer, which are loved by pollinators, including bees, butterflies and moths.

The plant also serves a dual purpose for painted lady butterflies, since the spiny, dark green leaves provide food for their caterpillars. The seed heads that develop after the flowers are rich in nutrients, too, and attract birds into the garden to feast on them in autumn and winter.

The plume thistle makes us happy because it is very easy to grow. Plant in any good garden soil, bar very dry or very wet, in a sunny spot and it will reward you with blooms animated with pollinators throughout mid- and late summer. The cultivar 'Atropurpureum' has richly coloured dark red blooms.

Traveller's joy

CLEMATIS VITALBA

Benefits
Pollinator plant; wildlife plant (food for caterpillars and birds)

Height & spread
Up to 6 x 1.5m (20 x 5ft)

A European native woodland plant, traveller's joy – or old man's beard as it's also known – scrambles up tall trees and weaves through hedgerows, the leafy, twining stems carrying clusters of small, creamy-white flowers, loved by pollinators, from midsummer to early autumn.

Hoverflies are particularly attracted to this plant's blooms, and their larvae eat unwanted insects such as aphids, providing you with a free natural pest control. The leaves support small emerald caterpillars and the buds and flowers nourish Haworth's pug moth caterpillars, while these larvae in turn offer food for birds. The wildlife benefits continue after flowering, too, as the silky seed heads – which resemble little beards, hence the name – help to sustain birds such as finches through the winter months.

Traveller's joy is a large, scrambling plant that needs space to ramble through a wildlife hedge or mature tree. Plant it in moist but well-drained soil in full sun or part shade, and prune all the stems down to 30cm (12in) above the ground in spring.

Foxglove

DIGITALIS

Benefits
Pollinator plant; wildlife plant (food for caterpillars)

Height & spread
90 x 50cm (36 x 20in)

Toxicity
All parts of this plant are poisonous

The much-loved foxglove is a staple of cottage and woodland gardens, its tall stems of colourful flowers drawing a host of pollinators into the garden when they appear in early summer.

Steeped in myths and symbolism, the plant is named after the tubular flowers, which look like tiny gloves, although it's not known exactly why they are associated with foxes. One story is that foxes wore the flowers on their paws so they could hunt silently, while another says that the plant grows at woodland edges where foxes make their dens.

The flowers have evolved to attract bees with long tongues, such as the common carder bee, and it is fascinating to watch these little insects land on the lower lip of a bloom, revealing the spotted interior that directs the insect inside to the nectar and pollen. Simply gazing at this performance is beneficial to our mental wellbeing, helping our brains to switch off and relax (see p.50), and because the pollen is so well protected and sticky, foxgloves are low-allergen plants and ideal for sufferers of hay fever.

Other insects that visit the plant include the foxglove pug moth, whose larvae crawl inside the flowers and eat the stamens and developing seeds – these caterpillars rarely do much damage, however, and help to increase the biodiversity in a garden.

Aside from these wildlife benefits, foxgloves contain a chemical called digitalin which, when properly extracted, is used in some drugs used to treat heart conditions, but remember that the plant is poisonous if eaten.

The most commonly grown foxglove is the biennial *Digitalis purpurea,* which you can sow from seed in spring. It will then develop leaves during its first summer, with flowers forming the following year. The plant prefers part shade and will grow in any good garden soil, bar waterlogged. Given the right conditions it may then self-seed in following years.

This group of plants includes short-lived perennials, too, such as *Digitalis lutea*, with its pale yellow flowers, which can be grown from seed and enjoys the same garden conditions as the biennial above.

Common teasel

DIPSACUS FULLONUM

Benefits
Decorative seed heads; pollinator plant; wildlife plant (food for birds)

Height & spread
Up to 90 x 50cm (36 x 20in)

This tall perennial plant gives joy to people and wildlife throughout the year, but particularly in winter, when its prickly seed heads offer food for birds and habitats for insects.

The teasel's spiny stems and green leaves with prickly midribs are joined from mid- to late summer by conical thistle-like flowerheads. These are green at first but then develop a halo of tiny purple blooms around the middle, the flowers gradually opening to cover the whole head. The blooms are loved by many pollinators, including bees, butterflies and moths, while the foliage attracts aphids, which in turn lure ladybirds and hoverflies into the garden, increasing its biodiversity.

The cone-shaped seed heads that follow the flowers in late summer and autumn offer a nutrient-rich larder for birds, which "tease" out the seeds with their beaks, hence the name. (Others say the name refers to the way in which seed heads were used to tease out the nap on fabrics.) The plant helps to sustain goldfinches, sparrows, buntings, robins, starlings, wagtails and other birds through winter and the aerial displays of wings and feathers hold our attention, allowing us to be present in the moment, free of other cares and worries. The prickly seed heads offer a snug hiding place for overwintering insects which, in turn, provide more food for birds.

Once dried, the seed heads add texture and interest to indoor dried flower arrangements and make beautiful Christmas decorations.

A native of Europe, Asia and North Africa, teasels are biennial, which means they germinate and produce leaves in their first year, and flower and set seed in their second. Any seeds not eaten by wildlife soon germinate and you will find plants appearing all over the garden, so look out for the seedlings and remove any you don't want.

Sow the seed in spring directly into the ground, protecting it from birds with some netting, or sow in pots of peat-free seed compost. Plants are not too fussy about soil conditions and will thrive in most types, bar waterlogged, and in full sun or partial shade.

Lady's eardrops

FUCHSIA MAGELLANICA

Benefits
Pollinator plant; wildlife plant (food for birds)

Height & spread
Up to 2.5 x 1.2m (8 x 4ft)

When they appear in summer, the dainty flowers of lady's eardrops twirl on slender stems like tiny ballerinas, demanding our attention and that of passing pollinators, which are attracted to their stores of nectar and pollen.

While most tender fuchsias are used for hanging basket and summer container displays, this medium-sized, relatively hardy shrub makes a wonderful, long-flowering plant for a bed or border. Its flowers comprise outer scarlet sepals (petal-like structures) that protect the purple tubular flowers with their long pistils and stamens. The blooms are designed to attract long-tongued bees, butterflies and moths and offer these pollinators food throughout late summer and autumn, when native flowers have largely been and gone. Other fuchsias have evolved for hummingbird pollination.

The large, eye-catching elephant hawk moth, a native of the UK and Europe, is a particular fan of this plant's flowers. However, this is unusual because fuchsias hail from Argentina, Chile and South America, but scientists believe these insects like them because the plants are closely related to the moth's favourite food, the native rosebay willowherb (*Chamaenerion angustifolium*), and probably taste very similar.

This shrub is one of the hardiest fuchsias and while the species is pink and purple, there are many forms to choose from, offering a wide range of flower colours and combinations – select those with single flowers for wildlife. The flowers are followed by small, edible berries, which are eaten by some birds.

Plant in a moist but well-drained soil in dappled shade and don't worry if the shrub dies back during a cold winter – new shoots will appear in spring. However, a protective mulch of bark chips will help to provide insulation for young plants, while their roots establish.

Ice plant

HYLOTELEPHIUM SPECTABILE

Benefits
Decorative seed heads; pollinator plant; wildlife plant (food and habitats)

Height & spread
Up to 90 x 50cm (36 x 20in)

Known to many by its former name, *Sedum spectabile*, this easy-going perennial is a must for anyone wishing to support wildlife in their garden, and to enjoy the long-lasting flowers that open from late summer to mid-autumn.

The ice plant is a magnet for butterflies, which has given rise to the plant's other common name, the butterfly stonecrop. These colourful insects love this plant, which hails from China and Korea. As the green buds open to reveal the tiny flowers, you can enjoy a fascinating display of small tortoiseshells, peacocks and red admirals stocking up on nectar before they find a sheltered site to overwinter. Other pollinators, including all manner of bees and hoverflies, are drawn to the flat-topped flowerheads, but choose the old-fashioned pink species to attract them, since white and red cultivars are not as alluring.

Leave the dark brown seed heads to stand over winter, where they will provide a habitat for insects, which birds will feast on as they emerge in spring. The seed heads inject much-needed interest into the winter garden, too, when our moods can flag if there is nothing to draw us outside.

Ice plants are the perfect choice for time-poor gardeners and those with small spaces to fill. The knee-high perennials, with their grey-green fleshy leaves, are very drought-tolerant once established and support the most insects when grown in full sun, although they will tolerate light shade. Plant them in spring, and water well until they are established – if, after a few years, the stems start to splay out, cut them back by half in late spring, a technique known as the Chelsea chop, since pruning coincides with the RHS Chelsea Flower Show. Alternatively, in autumn or early spring, dig up and divide the plant into smaller clumps, discarding old stems and replanting the healthy divisions.

Oregon grape

MAHONIA × MEDIA

Benefits

Scented winter flowers; pollinator plant; wildlife plant (food for birds)

Height & spread

Up to 2.5 x 2.5m (8 x 8ft)

The spiny leaves of this decorative evergreen shrub provide year-round interest in the garden, while its spikes of sweetly scented, yellow winter flowers offer early-flying bees sustenance when little else is in bloom.

The popular form of Oregon grape, *Mahonia* × *media* 'Charity', is loved for its long stems of holly-like, prickly evergreen foliage, but it is during winter that the plant comes into its own, arresting us with its clusters of perfumed flowers as we walk outside, and announcing to early-flying pollinators that nectar and pollen are on the menu.

The blooms are followed by decorative blue berries, which are loved by birds – blackbirds are especially partial to the nutrient-rich fruits.

This large shrub needs space to extend its long, leafy stems, and a spot where the spiny foliage will not snag clothing or cause harm. Ideal for a shady area that can be seen from a window, allowing you to enjoy it from indoors too, plant it where the scented flowers can be appreciated as you stroll through the garden in winter.

An easy-going plant, the Oregon grape is not particularly fussy about soil and will thrive even in the dry conditions beneath a tree. Prune back unwanted stems in spring, after flowering, to keep it in check.

In smaller spaces, try *Mahonia aquifolium*, which is more compact in size but offers similar wildlife benefits, its fragrant flowers appearing slightly later in spring.

Crab apple

MALUS 'EVERESTE'

Benefits
Autumn leaf colour; pollinator plant; wildlife plant (fruits eaten by birds, insects and mammals)

Height & spread
4 x 4m (13 x 13ft)

Trees offer many benefits for people and pollinators and this stunning crab apple is one of the best for both you and the wildlife in your garden. Few trees match it for the diversity of garden creatures it supports, and for the beautiful flowers, foliage and fruit.

A compact, deciduous tree, *Malus* 'Evereste' produces branches laden in spring with pollen- and nectar-rich flowers. Bright red in bud, they open to reveal the pure white blossom just as the glossy green leaves are unfurling. The foliage then turns a buttery yellow in autumn as the little orange fruits that follow the flowers are ripening, ready to be picked off by birds, including blackbirds and thrushes, later in the winter. Mammals, including mice, voles and foxes, are partial to the small fruits that fall to the ground.

While all crab apples are edible, if quite sour, the small fruits of this species are a bit too fiddly to core and make into jellies and preserves, so try 'Dartmouth' or 'John Downie' if you want to use them in this way.

Crabs get their name from the gnarled, twisted stems that develop on mature trees, and they are among the few trees that play host to mistletoe, *Viscum album,* a parasitic plant associated with happy Christmas celebrations. Crevices in the bark also harbour insects that provide food for birds, while the leaves of crab apples support the caterpillars of many moths, including the eyed hawkmoth, green pug and pale tussock.

This compact tree is ideal for small town gardens since it is tolerant of air pollution, while in a more open site in the countryside, it will withstand an exposed, cold spot. Plant it in full sun or part shade in any garden soil, bar waterlogged.

Tobacco plant

NICOTIANA

Benefits
Pollinator plant

Height & spread
Up to 1.5 x 0.6m (5 x 2ft)

This night-scented plant is perfect for a patio pot or for adding colour and fragrance to a border, and, like many flowers that come into their own as the sun sets, it has evolved to attract moths.

When we think of pollinators, bees and butterflies spring to mind, but moths perform an equally important job. There are estimated to be around 160,000 species of moths worldwide, and they are known as indicator species, which means their population sizes reflect the health of an ecosystem, so lots of moths in your garden means it is providing a good home for wildlife. Moths also sustain bats.

Tobacco plants range in size, with taller species, such as the white-flowered *Nicotiana sylvestris*, growing to over 1m (3ft) tall, while cultivars of *N. alata* may reach just 30cm (12in). All are annuals and easy to grow from seed in pots or trays of peat-free seed compost in spring. However, they are not hardy and must be kept inside until all threat of frost has passed in late spring, after which they can be planted outside in full sun or light shade in any garden soil, apart from waterlogged, or in a container of peat-free compost.

Evening primrose

OENOTHERA BIENNIS

Benefits
Pollinator plant; wildlife plant (food for birds)

Height & spread
Up to 1.5 x 0.6m (5 x 2ft)

Evening primrose is a wonderful plant for night-flying insects such as moths, which are attracted to its bowl-shaped, fragrant yellow flowers that appear throughout the summer and autumn.

Bees are also lured to the nectar and pollen, while the scent and activity of the insects hard at work will help you to relax on a warm summer's evening.

The seeds are eaten by birds, and the oil extracted from them has long been used to treat a wide range of health conditions, including eczema and premenstrual tension (PMT). It also helps to maintain good bone health.

Easy to grow from seed in spring in pots or sow directly in the ground, this hardy biennial will produce leaves in the first year and flowers in the second. Plant in full sun and well-drained soil for the best results.

Oak tree

QUERCUS

Benefits
Wildlife plant (food for insects, birds and bats)

Height & spread
Up to 40 x 15m (130 x 50ft)

A familiar site in woodlands and forests, the mighty English oak (*Quercus robur*) supports over 2,000 species of flora and fauna in Europe, while the white oak (*Quercus alba*) performs an equally important role in North America.

Oak trees provide a habitat for many insects, the leaves and flower buds supplying food to a range of butterfly and moth caterpillars, while other invertebrates hide in the crevices in the bark. Together, these creatures offer a nutritious menu for birds seeking protein-rich foods to feed their young in spring and summer. In autumn, blue jays, woodpeckers and nuthatches, and, of course, squirrels, eat the acorns, while the boughs and trunks provide nesting sites for all manner of wildlife, including bats, as well as birds.

The reddish-brown foliage that falls from the tree in autumn creates yet another important habitat, the distinctive, wavy-edged leaves breaking down to support invertebrates such as beetles, and providing ideal conditions for many fungi.

Although far too big for most gardens, mature oak trees are important wildlife habitats, and if you do have the space, they offer many rewards, including shelter and shade. For those with small gardens, you may be lucky enough to have an oak tree already growing close to your garden that you can enjoy, or visit local parks and countryside to appreciate these beautiful trees – the exercise, birdsong (see pp.42–43) and wildlife all contribute to overall wellbeing. Collecting the acorns is also fun for children, and they can be used as decorations and in various games such as "aim and toss", where you throw the nuts into a series of buckets and jars.

If you can accommodate an oak, buy bare-root young trees from late autumn to late winter, and plant in a sunny or partly shaded area in any garden soil, bar waterlogged. The tree takes about 40 years to start producing acorns and many more than that to reach its full height, so buy an older tree if you want to enjoy the nuts, or be patient and consider it a gift for your children and grandchildren to enjoy.

Scabious

SCABIOSA

Benefits
Pollinator plant; wildlife plant (food for birds)

Height & spread
Up to 90 x 60cm (3 x 2ft); smaller forms are available

Often referred to as pincushions, thanks to their little domed flowers with small pin-like stamens, scabious attract a wide range of bees, butterflies and moths that lift our mood as we watch them darting from bloom to bloom.

There are many species of scabious, but the most widely grown is the small scabious, *Scabiosa columbaria*, a native of the UK, Europe, Africa and western Asia, and *Scabiosa caucasica*, which hails from the warmer climes in Europe and is not quite as hardy. There are also many cultivars grown from these and others, and all offer long-lasting blooms that are rich in nectar and attract pollinators from summer through to the autumn. The seeds of *Scabiosa columbaria* provide food for birds, too.

The devil's bit scabious *(Succisa pratensis)* is a different species but equally valuable to wildlife. The spherical purple flowers held on tall stems are particularly loved by hoverflies, and the leaves offer food for moth and butterfly larvae. Birds also enjoy the seeds that follow the blooms in autumn.

The blue- and purple-flowered forms of both plants are calming (see also pp.44 and 50), helping us to relax, and they are very easy to grow, making them ideal for new gardeners. Grow *Scabiosa* species from seed or buy young plants in spring and offer them a site in full sun and free-draining soil – the compact types look beautiful in pots of peat-free compost. The devil's bit scabious thrives in the damp soil beside a pond or stream, or a marshy meadow, and grows well in full sun or part shade.

Dandelion

TARAXACUM OFFICINALE

Benefits
Pollinator plant; wildlife plant (food for birds)

Height & spread
20 x 20cm
(8 x 8in)

The dandelion is an important plant for pollinators, and while you may not want your lawn awash with its yellow flowers, consider keeping a few plants in a quiet area, where they will help to support more than 50 species of insect, including bees, butterflies and wasps.

Wasps may not seem like desirable insects, but they actually play an important role in the garden ecosystem. Just nine of the 250 species of wasp actually sting, and of those, most only do so in defence, while the remaining species are non-aggressive. In spring, wasps' larvae consume aphids and other unwanted insects that munch on our flowers and crops.

Birds also feast on dandelion seed, which is another reason to save a few plants, while the seed heads are enjoyed by children. Blowing on their "clocks", and making a wish as they float into the air, helps to nurture a love of plants and nature in young ones that carries through into adulthood.

The flowers are edible and make a soothing tea, while the buds can be used as an alternative to capers. Dandelion roots have long been harvested to flavour soft drinks and can be dried and roasted to make a caffeine-free coffee substitute, which is a natural diuretic. You won't need to buy dandelions as they will find their way into most gardens, so simply leave them to do their own thing and the wildlife will follow.

Stinging nettle

URTICA DIOICA

Benefits
Wildlife plant (food for birds)

Height & spread
Up to 1.2 x 2.5m (4 x 8ft)

The stinging nettle is another species that many people would not think of as beneficial, but it plays a crucial role in the garden ecosystem, and while being stung by a nettle won't make you laugh, the plant makes many insects very happy.

Nettles offer food for red admiral, comma, peacock and small tortoiseshell butterfly larvae and when the caterpillars metamorphose into the beautiful, winged adults, they will definitely bring joy into your life. These fascinating insects help our brains to switch off for a few moments as we watch their aerial displays and inspect their intricately patterned wings when they pause to feed.

Nettles' catkin-like flowers are followed by seed heads that support birds, and you may also spot ladybirds enjoying the aphids the plants often harbour.

Stinging nettles will take up home in a suitable spot in your garden of their own accord, so just nurture a few plants in a quiet corner when they appear.

The joy of veg

Eating a diet rich in vegetables will help to improve our health, while a few edibles have special powers to boost physical and mental wellbeing, some in surprising ways.

Broccoli 'Beneforte'

BRASSICA OLERACEA ITALICA GROUP 'BENEFORTE'

Benefits
Pollinator plant; flowers and stems contain glucosinolates and help protect against disease

Height & spread
Up to 60 x 60cm (24 x 24in)

Dubbed "super broccoli", 'Beneforte' is a crop you will want to grow to keep both you and your family happy and healthy.

A cross between commercial varieties and wild broccoli, this form contains two to three times more glucosinolates, a compound present in all brassicas which is thought to protect against cancer, heart disease and diabetes.

The good news doesn't stop there, either, since dietary studies suggest that eating glucosinolates on a regular basis boosts our natural defence systems, keeping us functioning well as we age.

Eat the whole plant, too, not just the flowerheads. Chop up the stems and add them to the menu, since they are high in dietary fibre, which helps to maintain good gut health. The microbes in the gut have a huge influence on both our mental and physical wellbeing, and research shows that eating a diet rich in lots of different vegetables and fruits can reduce symptoms of anxiety and depression, too.

Other brassicas to grow that have similar benefits include kale, Savoy cabbage and Brussels sprouts.

Broccoli is relatively easy to grow, if you have a patch of well-drained soil in sun or part shade. Sow seeds in pots of peat-free seed compost under cover in spring and plant the seedlings outside from mid-spring, about 45cm (18in) apart. Protect the developing seedlings from cabbage white butterflies and cabbage moths with fine-mesh butterfly netting, ensuring that it does not touch the plants. Crops will be ready to harvest from midsummer to mid-autumn.

You could leave a few plants to "bolt", or flower, since the blooms help to sustain pollinators and the subsequent seeds are eaten by birds.

Chilli pepper

CAPSICUM

Benefits
Decorative fruits; fruits contain vitamin C and capsaicin, and protect against disease

Height & spread
About 60 x 30cm (24 x 12in)

Growing a couple of chilli pepper plants on a sunny kitchen windowsill or in a greenhouse will brighten your home or garden with spicy, jewel-coloured fruits from midsummer to late autumn.

Chilli fruits come in a wide range of shapes and colours, including green, red, purple, orange and yellow. You can select from mild to hot and spicy flavours – in general, the larger the fruit, the milder the taste. The colourful peppers have many health benefits and offer among the highest levels of antioxidants of any fruit or vegetable, with red and purple varieties topping the bill.

The active ingredient in chillies is capsaicin, which makes them taste hot and burns our tongues, but it also helps to protect us from cancer and some diseases, including diabetes. Capsaicin may even help you to lose weight. Studies show that it reduces appetite and may increase metabolism, helping you to burn off calories. The highest level of capsaicin is found in the hottest chillies – measured in Scoville heat units (SHU) – but all types offer the benefits to some degree.

Raw chillies are packed with more vitamin C than oranges, helping to keep the skin and nervous system healthy. They also contain vitamin A, needed for eye health, and iron, which protects against anaemia and wards off disease by strengthening the immune system.

The plants are easy to grow in containers of peat-free potting compost. Sow from seed or buy a few young plants in spring and keep them well watered. Originally from South and Central America, chilli plants are not hardy and in cold climates they must be kept indoors until all threat of frost has passed in late spring. However, plants may fruit better on a bright, sunny windowsill indoors or in a greenhouse during cool summers.

Pumpkin

CUCURBITA

Benefits
Pollinator plant; fruits contain vitamins C and E, protect against disease and promote good eye health

Height & spread
Up to 0.5 x 2.5m (20in x 8ft)

As the days shorten and winter approaches, our moods can take a plunge, but the bright orange skins of ripe pumpkins ready to harvest lift the spirits, while their sweet flesh offers the promise of many delicious dishes to savour.

Many pumpkins are ideal for eating, but we can't ignore the large carving types that provide hours of fun during the run-up to Halloween. This mindful activity helps us to relax and enjoy the time spent together during the celebrations.

Good choices of eating pumpkins are *Cucurbita maxima* 'Red Kuri' (also known as 'Uchiki Kuri'), a small-fruiting variety with an orange skin and nutty flavour; 'Crown Prince', with its pale grey-blue skins and bright orange flesh; and the small, dark green *C. sativus* 'Bonbon', which has bright orange, sweet flesh. For carving, opt for the traditional large orange-skinned varieties of *Cucurbita pepo*, such as 'Jack o' Lantern' and 'Prizewinner', or the smaller 'Baby Bear'.

If you have space, grow one or two of both, as the health benefits of the fruits are not to be missed. They are rich sources of various minerals and vitamins, including vitamins C and E, which help to strengthen the immune system, and also contain the antioxidant beta-carotene, which helps to protect against heart disease and some cancers. When eaten, it converts to vitamin A and lutein, which improve vision and promote good eye health, while offering anti-ageing skin benefits. The seeds are nutritious, too, and help maintain a healthy gut. All these benefits, and the flesh is delicious – what's not to like?

Grow pumpkins from seed in spring, planting them in pots of peat-free seed compost indoors and planting out the seedlings when all risk of frost has passed in late spring. Pumpkins prefer a fertile, moist soil and full sun for their skins to ripen. Their long, trailing stems, large leaves and fruits require space to grow, although small-fruiting varieties can be trained up sturdy trellis or along wires.

Carrot

DAUCUS CAROTA* SUBSP. *SATIVUS

Benefits
Pollinator plant; roots contain vitamin A, protect against disease and promote good eye health

Height & spread
50 x 20cm (20 x 8in)

Remember when your grandma told you to eat carrots if you wanted to see in the dark? Well, it turns out that this old tale has a lot of truth to it.

Scientific studies have shown these sweet roots contain a vitamin that does, in fact, help to improve night vision and is very good for our eye health in general. Seeing clearly is definitely a reason to celebrate.

Carrots contain a range of health-boosting plant chemicals (phytochemicals), including beta-carotene, which converts to vitamin A and lutein, both of which promote good eye health (see also p.105). If you grow yours from seed, you can select purple carrots, which contain anthocyanins, a pigment that has been shown to help protect against heart disease, some cancers and Alzheimer's disease. Put some red carrots on the menu and you can add another phytochemical known as lycopene to the mix, which offers the benefits already listed, as well as promoting healthy skin (see also p.110).

Looking good and feeling fit are just some of the benefits of eating a diet rich in carrots, but steam or bake them, rather than eating them raw, since this helps us to digest them and absorb the vitamins and phytochemicals they contain.

Growing carrots is relatively easy. Sow the seed in small batches from midspring to midsummer in a sunny site and on free-draining soil. You can also sow them in large pots. Thin out the seedlings, if necessary, so that plants are about 5–7.5cm (2–3in) apart. Protect your plants from carrot fly, whose larvae feed on the roots, covering your crops with insect-proof mesh and ensuring that it does not touch the plants.

French bean

PHASEOLUS VULGARIS

Benefits
Pollinator plant; pods contain folate, protect against disease and promote sleep

Height & spread
Up to 4 x 0.9m (13 x 3ft); bush varieties are smaller

French beans are a great crop for a small garden, the twining stems of climbers or compact dwarf varieties providing a good supply of pods, while taking up little space on the ground.

These tasty vegetables are packed with health-promoting antioxidants, including vitamin C, flavonoids, quercetin and kaempferol, which offer protection against some cancers and help to reduce "bad" cholesterol. French beans are rich in fibre, which is good for gut health, and they are easily digested, allowing people with irritable bowel disease (IBS) to eat them without discomfort.

For mothers-to-be, a portion of French beans provides about one-third of the daily recommended intake of folate, a B vitamin important for the growth and development of unborn babies. This same vitamin helps to support mental wellbeing, reducing depression by increasing the production of serotonin, dopamine and norepinephrine, hormones that regulate mood and appetite, and help us to sleep. These beans contain vitamin K and some calcium, both of which help maintain strong bones and reduce the risk of fractures. So, for health and happiness, grow a few beans.

Growing your own means you can opt for "Purple podded" beans, too, which add colour to the vegetable garden and offer the benefits of green beans, plus anthocyanins. These are pigments that give fruits, flowers and leaves their red, purple and blue colour, and help to reduce inflammation and protect against diabetes and heart disease.

Sow the beans in pots of peat-free seed compost indoors from mid- to late spring, or directly outside after the frosts in fertile, moisture-retentive soil and full sun. Grow climbing varieties up tall supports such as wigwams made from canes or prunings, or try dwarf varieties in large pots of peat-free compost. Keep plants well-watered, and when the pods appear, pick them regularly to encourage more to form.

Oyster mushroom

PLEUROTUS OSTREATUS

Benefits
Contain B vitamins, promote good skin and eye health, and help alleviate depression

Height & spread
n/a

Technically fungi and not vegetables, these large, meaty mushrooms are delicious and beneficial to our health and happiness. Found in the wild on dead or decaying logs in temperate and tropical forests, they can be grown at home from kits, either outside in the garden or indoors.

Some oyster mushroom kits will sprout these decorative fungi within weeks, to the delight of children and adults alike, who will be amazed by the speed with which they develop. The mushrooms have a mild flavour and meaty texture, and can be used in a range of savoury dishes, including stir-fries, soups, pastas and risottos. Also try grilling or roasting them to enhance their flavour and texture.

Scientists have found that oyster mushrooms contain higher levels of antioxidants than other mushrooms, making these the top choice for your health. Rich in B vitamins, including folate (see also p.109) which helps to regulate our moods and alleviates depression, they also contain vitamin E, an antioxidant that helps to maintain healthy skin and eyes, while strengthening the immune system. Edible mushrooms are the best source of the antioxidant ergothioneine, which may help to lower the risk of cancer, and the fibre they contain helps to promote good gut health and may lower cholesterol levels.

You can buy kits to grow oyster mushrooms indoors in bags or boxes that include fresh grain spawn. Some kits also use old coffee grounds, which provide the perfect medium for growing mushrooms, and once the kit is set up, you will be harvesting fresh fungi within a few weeks.

Outdoor kits comprise dowels inoculated with native mushroom mycelium, which you insert into a fresh log, seasoned for 2–6 weeks, in the garden. The log needs to be kept moist and set in a sheltered spot, out of direct sunlight. This is a longer-term method, with the first mushrooms appearing after about a year, but you will then be harvesting them for about three years after that.

Tomato

SOLANUM LYCOPERSICUM

Benefits
Decorative fruits; fruits contain lypocene, vitamins E, B, C and K, and protect against disease

Height & spread
Up to 2 x 0.6m (6ft 6in x 2ft)

The taste of a fresh, sweet tomato plucked from the vine in summer is bound to make you smile, especially if you have grown the fruit yourself. These little flavour bombs look beautiful, too, glistening like giant rubies in the sun.

Tomatoes are known as superfoods because of their many health-giving properties. They contain the phytochemicals lycopene and beta-carotene, which studies have shown help to prevent some cancers, especially prostate cancer. Lycopene is also associated with brain health, and may offer some protection against Alzheimer's disease, as well as helping to increase bone strength.

The fruits are good sources of vitamin E (see also p.110), B vitamins, including folate, which helps to improve mental wellbeing (see also p.109), vitamin C, vitamin K, and potassium and manganese, minerals that promote good heart and brain health. A scientific study found that drinking tomato juice helps muscles to recover after exercise, so have a glass when you have been to the gym or gone for a run, to prevent aches and pains.

The key nutrients and phytochemicals in tomatoes are more easily absorbed into the body when tomatoes are cooked, the heat breaking down their thick cell walls and releasing their goodness. Research shows that adding olive oil when cooking also helps the body to absorb more lycopene.

You can grow tomatoes from seed, which will offer you the widest choice of varieties, or buy young plants in spring. Tomatoes are not hardy, so keep the seedlings indoors until all risk of frost has passed. Some varieties are bred for growing outside in the garden, while others do best in a greenhouse, where they will be protected from blight, a fungal disease that can ruin the crop. Tomato plants need full sun and a moist but free-draining soil, or peat-free multipurpose compost if grown in a pot. Tie cordon tomatoes to a tall cane to support their stems, and remove side-shoots that appear between the main stem and side stems of these types.

An apple a day

Recent studies have shown that the old proverb about apples helping to keep the doctor away is actually true, while other fruits are also packed with nutrients and compounds that help to increase wellbeing.

Black chokeberry

ARONIA MELANOCARPA

Benefits
Autumn foliage colour; pollinator plant; wildlife plant (food for birds); berries contain vitamins C and B, protect against disease, and support mental health

Height & spread
1.5 x 1.5m (5 x 5ft)

You may not have heard of the black chokeberry, but this decorative fruit bush has a place in our list of happy plants because it is both easy to grow and delivers a host of health benefits.

The medium-sized to large shrub is a North American native and gets its name from the astringent fruits, which can be a little unpalatable when eaten raw, but taste delicious in jams, jellies and teas.

Scientific studies show that chokeberries have the highest polyphenol content of any berry. Polyphenols are plant-based compounds that have health-giving properties and these glossy black fruits may offer protection against a wide range of illnesses, including heart disease and some cancers, including colon cancer. They also help to protect against stomach ulcers and are used in the treatment and prevention of diabetes.

Like most berries, chokeberries are a good source of vitamin C, essential for the health of our skin and nervous system, as well as B vitamins, including folate, which helps to support mental health (see also p.109). They also provide the minerals potassium, calcium, magnesium, iron and zinc that collectively support the health of our heart, blood, bones, nerves and muscles.

Other benefits to enjoy are the white flowers that appear in late spring and attract pollinators, while the fruits that follow provide food for birds as well as us humans. In addition, the plant lights up the garden in autumn when its green leaves turn bright red, just as the berries are ready to harvest.

Growing a chokeberry couldn't be easier. Plant the shrub in moist but well-drained soil – it thrives in acid soil but will cope in most types, except chalky – and in full sun or part shade.

Calamondin orange

CITRUS × MICROCARPA

Benefits
Fruits contain Vitamin C and potassium, and protect against disease

Height & spread
Up to 3 x 1.8m (10 x 6ft)

Growing a few citrus plants at home brings us great joy, as their scented flowers fill the air with fragrance and the vitamin-packed fruits deliver delicious sweet treats. Calamondin oranges are among the easiest to grow in cooler climes.

The desire to grow citrus fruits in Northern Europe has a long history and in the seventeenth century wealthy aristocrats built special extensions to their mansions with large windows, known as orangeries, designed to protect their precious plants in winter. Today, citrus fruit trees are just as popular, their flowers and ornamental fruits creating a talking point, while oranges' fragrance is used in aromatherapy to relieve depression, reduce stress and promote a good night's sleep.

In a cool climate, some citrus trees can be challenging to maintain, but one of the easiest to grow is the calamondin. A hybrid of a mandarin orange and kumquat, it produces small orange fruits, which have a bitter taste at first, but then sweeten in the mouth and are ideal for making marmalade.

The fruits are an excellent source of vitamin C and antioxidants, including flavonoids, which may reduce the risk of chronic diseases, including some cancers. They also contain potassium, which helps regulate blood pressure, and offer a source of fibre, essential for good gut health.

Plant your calamondin in a large pot filled with a mix of peat-free soil-based compost and ericaceous compost, and keep it in a cool, sunny room from autumn to spring if you live in a frost-prone area. A centrally heated room will not be suitable. Water plants sparingly in winter, ideally with rain or filtered water, and feed with a citrus fertilizer designed for winter growth, following the application rates and timings on the packaging.

The plant will then benefit from a summer holiday in the garden in a sunny spot, but do ensure its pot has drainage holes in the bottom, and bring it indoors again before the frosts in autumn. Feed at this time of year with citrus fertilizer for summer growth. The fruit takes a year to mature and will be ready to harvest at the same time as the flowers appear in late winter or early spring.

Apple tree

MALUS DOMESTICA

Benefits
Pollinator plant; wildlife plant (fruit is food for insects, mammals and birds); fruits support gut health and protect against disease

Height & spread
Up to 4 x 4m (13 x 13ft)

The old saying that an apple a day keeps the doctor away has, say scientists, a lot of truth to it, and the sweet fruits have been shown to help reduce the risk of heart disease and cancer, while boosting gut health.

The trees themselves also make us and our garden wildlife happy. An apple tree in bloom on a sunny day in spring lifts our spirits and attracts a host of pollinating insects such as honeybees, bumblebees and hoverflies, while the branches offer birds nesting and roosting sites. As the year turns, their boughs offer cool shade during the hotter months, and in early to mid-autumn they deliver their harvest of sweet fruits. Butterflies and a variety of birds, including thrushes and blackbirds, also enjoy the fallen fruits.

These are just some reasons to grow an apple tree, but there are more. The health benefits are derived from the pectin found in the fruits. This is a type of dietary fibre that supports gut health and may offer protection against cancer, heart disease and asthma. Red-skinned varieties such as 'Pink Lady' and 'Red Falstaff' also contain anthocyanins, which promote good health (see also p.106), while 'Redlove', with its pink flesh, has a 40 per cent higher antioxidant content than the average apple. Eating the whole fruit, including the skin, is best for your health.

Apple trees can be bought as bare-root plants from late autumn to early spring. Choose a variety grown on a rootstock that will suit the size of your plot. For example, an M26 rootstock will make a compact tree about 2.5m (8ft) high, while an MM106 will make a medium-sized tree about 4m (13ft) tall. You can then choose the fruit type such as 'Cox's Orange Pippin', 'Discovery' or 'Bramley's Seedling'. Plant in a sunny site in any good garden soil, bar waterlogged; for more information on planting, visit rhs.org.uk and search for "planting fruit trees".

Plum tree

PRUNUS DOMESTICA

Benefits
Pollinator plant; wildlife plant (food for insects, mammals and birds); fruits contain vitamin C and protect against disease

Height & spread
Up to 4 x 4m (13 x 13ft)

Trees adorned with ripe plums in late summer will lift your spirits and tantalize your taste buds when harvested to eat fresh or to make into jams, pies, puddings, drinks and savoury sauces.

The trees have many attributes that add interest to the garden, their scented white blossom attracting a host of pollinators, including butterflies, bees and moths, who together ensure a bumper crop of sweet fruits. Suitable for small gardens, plum trees offer shade in summer, and the fruits that ripen later in the season come in a choice of black, blue, purple, red or yellow varieties.

Plums are quite expensive to buy at the supermarket, but in most summers a mature tree will provide you with bowls of fruit at no cost, and the health benefits you will derive from eating these sweet treats will tempt you further. The best varieties for health are red- and purple-skinned plums, which contain high levels of the polyphenols, anthocyanins and carotenoids that deliver protection against heart disease and some cancers (see also p.106). They are also a good source of fibre, essential for good gut health, and vitamin C, which helps to keep eyes and skin healthy. Scientific research into dried plums, or prunes, also suggests that they help to increase bone strength, and may improve memory and cognitive skills.

To enjoy the health benefits, eat the plums when they are fully ripe, since the polyphenols increase as the skin colours up. Birds are also attracted to the fruits, and may sample some of your crop, but there is usually enough for everyone and the benefits wildlife provides for mental wellbeing make them welcome visitors to the garden (see also p.43).

Choose a tree of the eventual size and variety you require and plant in full sun and moist, but well-drained soil, ideally in an area protected from heavy frosts, since trees blossom quite early in spring and a cold snap can damage the flowers. For more advice on planting plum trees, visit rhs.org.uk and search for "growing plum trees".

Blackcurrant

RIBES NIGRUM

Benefits
Pollinator plant; wildlife plant (food for birds); currants contain vitamin C and protect against disease

Height & spread
1.5 x 1.5m (5 x 5ft)

Time-poor gardeners searching for an easy crop that will deliver a harvest of tangy fruits with a range of health benefits should look no further than juicy, nutrient-packed blackcurrants.

The health benefits of blackcurrants are well-known, the fruits packed with vitamin C and polyphenols, including anthocyanins and flavanols, which protect against heart disease and some cancers. The oil derived from the currants is also used to treat eczema and skin conditions, while tea made from the leaves may help to lower blood pressure.

The spring flowers offer pollinators a rich store of nectar and pollen, and birds also enjoy the berries, which may mean protecting most of your bushes with a fruit cage or birdproof netting, as they are apt to take the lot.

You will need space to grow the shrubs, which reach about 1.5m (5ft) in height and spread, but once planted, they require little attention and will crop year after year, keeping both you and the local wildlife happy. In smaller gardens, look out for standard-trained blackcurrants, which grow on a single stem topped with a lollipop-shaped fruiting crown.

Plant blackcurrants in a sunny or partly shaded spot, in any good garden soil, bar waterlogged. Once established, prune the fruited stems in winter. For more advice on blackcurrants, visit rhs.org.uk and search for “growing blackcurrants”.

Benefits
Pollinator plant; wildlife plant (food for birds); berries contain vitamin C and protect against disease

Height & spread
2.5 x 2.5m (8 x 8ft)

Blackberry

RUBUS FRUTICOSUS

Blackberries couldn't be easier to grow and the modern, thornless varieties such as 'Loch Ness' and 'Black Satin', which produce large, sweet fruits, are delicious when eaten fresh from the bush or made into jams and pies.

The berries are little health packages, offering all the benefits of other dark-coloured fruits, such as blackcurrants, together with more of the polyphenol ellagitannins than most. This antioxidant reduces inflammation and may help to fight bacterial infections and protect against some cancers. Raspberries and strawberries are other good sources. Blackberries also provide insoluble fibre, which maintains gut health and can protect against diabetes.

Grow blackberries in a sunny or partly shaded area and any garden soil, bar waterlogged. In small gardens, train the long stems on wires up a wall, or along a framework of wires stretched between sturdy poles on an allotment. The stems fruit on two-year-old growth; prune the fruited stems after harvest, retaining the new stems to fruit the following year.

Common elder

SAMBUCUS NIGRA

Benefits
Wildlife plant (food for birds); fruits contain vitamin C and protect against disease

Height & spread
Up to 6 x 6 metres (20 x 20ft), but can be kept smaller

Toxicity
Raw berries are mildly toxic

Few trees deliver as many benefits to wildlife and to our health and happiness as the common elder, its flowers harvested to make elderflower tea, cordial, wine or even a fizzy "champagne" to help soothe sore throats and sinus conditions.

This European native, with its attractive divided leaves, grows wild in hedgerows and at the edges of woodlands, where it provides a habitat for wildlife. The foliage supports many moth caterpillars, including the white-spotted pug, swallowtail, dot moth and buff ermine, while the boughs offer some shade and nesting sites for birds, and the young, hollow stems create shelter for overwintering insects and nests for solitary bees.

The elder produces flat heads of small, fragrant, cream flowers in early summer, followed by clusters of glistening black berries packed with goodness from late summer to early autumn. The fruits contain high levels of polyphenols, including flavanols and anthocyanins, which have many benefits, such as helping to protect against heart disease and some cancers, while supporting the immune system (see also p.106). However, remember to cook the berries before eating them, since they are mildly toxic when raw.

Birds such as blackbirds, song thrushes and redwings are also partial to the berries, but trees do not need to be covered because there are usually enough fruits to share, and birds also help to boost mental wellbeing as we watch their activities and enjoy their songs (see also p.43).

Elder is easy to grow and thrives in full sun or part shade and any garden soil, bar very dry or very wet. The trees can also be grown as part of a wildlife hedge, and cultivars with dark purple and variegated foliage are also available.

Pollution busters

While all plants help to reduce polluting carbon dioxide levels in the atmosphere, a few have additional powers to fight pollution and mitigate its negative effects on our health and the environment.

Franchet's cotoneaster

COTONEASTER FRANCHETII

Benefits
Pollinator plant; wildlife plant (food for birds); leaves trap airborne pollution particles

Height & spread
Up to 4 x 4m (13 x 13ft) if grown as a hedge

If you live near a busy road, this beautiful evergreen cotoneaster is the shrub for you. Dubbed a "superplant" by RHS scientists, it has a special ability to capture airborne pollution.

Franchet's cotoneaster has the power to make you happy in many ways, adding colour and structure to the garden with its red-tinted white summer flowers and bright orange-red berries in autumn, set against a backdrop of grey-green leaves. However, for those who suffer from asthma and allergies, conditions exacerbated by pollution, it has another important benefit, since research shows that the hairs on its leaves trap harmful airborne particles found in vehicle exhaust emissions. A few shrubs offer similar benefits, but this particular cotoneaster was found to be 20 per cent more effective than the others in the RHS study, mopping up the same amount of pollution in seven days that a car emits in a 500-mile drive.

Researchers recommend planting it as a hedge along busy roads in pollution hotspots. Alternatively, include it as part of a mixed hedge comprising different species in quieter areas, where it will support pollinators drawn to its nectar-rich flowers, and increase biodiversity.

This hardy Chinese native is easy to grow in the garden, and will thrive in any soil, bar waterlogged, in a sunny or partly shaded site. To grow it as a hedge, buy young plants in late autumn and plant them in a single row, about 40–60cm (20–24in) apart. Trim in late winter or early spring, once the plants have reached their desired height. When mature, hedges can be clipped at any time either side of birds' nesting season from spring to midsummer, but try to leave it large enough to flower and to produce the decorative berries, which are attractive to birds.

Sunflower

HELIANTHUS ANNUUS

Benefits
Pollinator plant; wildlife plant (food for birds); plants extract pollutants from the soil

Height & spread
Up to 2.5 x 0.6m (8 x 2ft), many cultivars are smaller

The classic shape of a sunflower and its bright yellow petals bring cheer, but this annual plant, grown by school children all over the world, has another surprising attribute that helps to create a healthy environment.

Known as a hyperaccumulator plant, the sunflower absorbs dangerous heavy metals in the soil, transporting them into its stems, leaves and flowerheads in a process called phytoremediation. Sunflowers were used to clean contaminated ground following the Chernobyl disaster of 1986, where fields of the flowers were planted to mop up the radioactive metals in the soil. After they had flowered, the plants were then harvested and disposed of safely in hazardous waste landfills designed to prevent leaching.

As well as radioactive metals, sunflowers are hyperaccumulators of many other heavy metal pollutants, including lead, cadmium, copper, nickel and zinc, and have been used to make soils contaminated with them safe near a Chrysler automotive production facility in Detroit.

However, it seems that not all sunflowers are equally effective, and when they were planted near the site of the Fukushima nuclear accident in Japan in 2011, they were not as successful in clearing the soil. Studies are ongoing into which flowers work best in these situations.

Garden soils are unlikely to be contaminated with dangerous levels of harmful metals, and if they were, you would need to dispose of your sunflowers in a special facility. However, they are fun and easy to grow from seed in pots or trays of peat-free seed compost; plant seedlings outside in a sunny site and free-draining soil, or a large pot.

Sweet pea

LATHYRUS ODORATUS

Benefits
Scented flowers; reduces carbon pollution when grown as cut flower

Height & spread
2.5 x 0.6m (8 x 2ft)

The captivating, scented flowers of the sweet pea have been grown for centuries for bridal bouquets and indoor arrangements, and planting a few in your garden to use in this way can help to reduce pollution levels.

While these colourful blooms do not absorb pollution like some other plants, growing them, together with other cut flowers, will help to reduce your carbon footprint. Many of the flowers we buy for our homes travel thousands of miles across the world to reach us. Roses often journey from Kenya to Amsterdam and then to various markets in Europe, while Columbia and Ecuador are the biggest exporters of blooms to the United States. According to research by the RHS, growing your own cut flowers can save up to 7.9kg (17lb) of CO_2 per bunch, compared to buying imported flowers, which is equivalent to the carbon cost of driving from London to Edinburgh and back nearly twice.

There is a current movement promoting the benefits of locally grown cut flowers that have been raised on farms closer to home, but an even better way to cut pollution from road transport and air cargo is to grow blooms right outside your door. Sweet peas are a strong contender because they produce flowers over many months if you pick them regularly. These climbers also make a beautiful feature in the garden, their twining stems of fragrant flowers covering obelisks and tripods to provide punctuation points in a bed or border. The colour range is huge, too, with flowers available in almost every shade under the sun. Another benefit is the price, since a packet of seeds is about the cost of a cup of coffee.

Sow them in deep pots of peat-free compost in autumn and overwinter them in a sheltered spot outside or a cool, bright room indoors, planting them out in spring in full sun and well-drained soil. Or sow the seed in spring for flowers a little later in the summer. You will need a framework of canes or a tall obelisk to grow them up. Once you're won over, try growing other cut flowers such as roses, sunflowers, dahlias and tulips.

Yew

TAXUS BACCATA

Benefits
Wildlife plant (food for birds); leaves trap airborne pollution particles

Height & spread
Up to 12 x 8m (40 x 26ft); hedging and topiary can be kept much smaller

Toxicity
All parts of the plant are toxic

Some of our oldest trees are yews, reaching an incredible 2,000 years of age or older. Known for their poisonous leaves and seeds encased in bright red berries, you may be wondering why these trees, often found in graveyards, would make us happy.

The yew gains its place within these pages because it helps to remove pollutants from the atmosphere, while providing a rich habitat for many birds and insects. Like *Cotoneaster fanchetti* (see also pp.130–1), yew foliage helps to capture airborne pollutants such as the small particles emitted from vehicle exhausts.

The needle-like evergreen leaves are not hairy, however, but coated with a layer of porous waxy cuticles that trap pollution particles. A study by researchers at the University of Surrey in the UK showed that evergreens with small leaves, such as yew, are particularly effective because they cling to pollution particles during windy conditions, and then allow rain to wash them safely to the ground, where they are less harmful. The study found yew to be the most effective at reducing airborne pollution of the evergreen plants tested.

Anyone growing yew must be mindful of the fact that all parts are poisonous, so it is not the best choice for gardens with young children or pets prone to chewing plants. However, for the rest of us, it is a good choice, not only offering protection against pollution but also providing birds with nesting sites and food, and offering sustenance for some moth caterpillars, including the satin beauty moth.

While yew is a large tree and not suitable for the average urban garden, hedging and topiary are popular options for plots of any size if they are trimmed annually in late summer. Buy bare-root yew hedging plants from late autumn to early spring and plant young trees 30cm (12in) apart in any good garden soil, bar waterlogged, in sun or shade.

Red clover

TRIFOLIUM PRATENSE

Benefits
Pollinator plant; absorbs the nutrient nitrogen to feed other plants

Height & spread
Up to 45 x 30cm (18 x 12in)

Red clover is a legume, a family of plants that also includes beans and peas, and it earns its place here because it can help to reduce the need for chemical fertilizers that contribute to pollution in rivers and oceans.

Red clover, like other legumes, has a special adaptation that allows bacteria on its roots to take the plant nutrient nitrogen from the atmosphere and convert it into a form that can sustain the plant's growth and health. Other plants must take up this vital nutrient, needed for photosynthesis and healthy foliage, from the soil. Nitrogen is the most ubiquitous gas in the air, comprising 78 per cent of the Earth's atmosphere, compared to oxygen at just 21 per cent, so red clover will never suffer from a deficiency.

Red clover can be used to feed other plants when it is grown as a "green manure", thereby reducing the need for chemical fertilizers. Start by sowing the seeds in spring or late summer or early autumn on beds where you will be growing hungry plants, such as vegetables. Once the clover plants have grown and flowered, cover them with a mulch, such as layers of cardboard topped with homemade compost, and leave them to rot down and enrich the soil. Alternatively, hoe off the top growth and leave it on the soil surface, then dig the plants into the top layers of soil. They will naturally deliver their package of nutrients there, promoting healthy crops and flowers.

You can also use clover to feed a lawn by sprinkling seeds over the grass in spring or autumn. It will then help to feed the plants around it, and it is drought-tolerant, remaining green throughout most summers. Lawns made exclusively from white clover (*Trifolium repens*) offer another easy-care option – the varieties 'Euromic' and 'Pipolina' are among the best choices for a clover lawn.

All clovers are rich in nectar and help to feed pollinators, and the plants can help to stabilize soils, protecting them from erosion.

Nasturtium

TROPAEOLUM MAJUS

Benefits
Pollinator plant; plants act as natural pesticides

Height & spread
30 x 60cm (12 x 24in)

The brightly coloured flowers of the nasturtium decorate summer borders and containers, while the edible foliage attracts aphids and can be used as a decoy to keep these insects off your crops.

This hardy annual is often used as a companion plant for roses, dahlias, broad beans and other crops susceptible to aphid attacks, luring these sap-sucking insects away from prized plants and reducing the need for human intervention. The cabbage white butterfly also lays its eggs on nasturtium leaves, as well as on cabbages and other brassicas, and nasturtiums grown close to these plants can help to act as decoys, although covering your crops with insect-proof netting is the most effective defence.

Acting as a decoy does, of course, mean that nasturtium plants themselves come under attack, but because they are so easy to grow from inexpensive seeds, you can afford to forfeit them. They also put on lots of growth during the summer months and can often sail through aphid infestations without too much damage, while also providing insect predators, such as ladybirds and their larvae and hoverfly larvae, with a meal of tasty aphids, their favourite food. So, you may find that your crops remain unharmed, while the nasturtiums also suffer less than expected as these predators polish off the sap-suckers.

Nasturtiums bring us joy in other ways, too, their bright orange, red and yellow flowers lifting our spirits. The plants attract a host of pollinators into the garden with their nectar-rich blooms, which help to keep us mindful as we watch their activities, increasing our mental wellbeing (see also p.50). The peppery-tasting leaves and blooms make a delicious addition to salads and stir fries, too.

To grow nasturtiums, sow seeds in pots of peat-free seed compost indoors in spring and plant out the seedlings once all risk of frost has passed in late spring. The plants thrive in well-drained soil and full sun, and the trailing stems can be trained up trellis or other supports.

Garden medicinals

Plants have long been used to treat a variety of ailments, while some provide the active ingredients in modern drug therapies, and those in this chapter are proven to increase our health and happiness.

ALLIUM SATIVUM

Benefits
Bulbs contain vitamins C and B, and protect against disease

Height & spread
30 x 15cm (12 x 6in)

This edible bulb has been used in folk medicine for centuries to treat colds, flu and a multitude of illnesses. As garlic is a good source of vitamin C and B vitamins, which help to bolster immunity, it may indeed help to fight infection, and recent research shows that it has other benefits, too.

Garlic contains fructans, which are good for gut health, and a sulphur compound called alliin, which converts to allicin, a powerful anti-inflammatory, when crushed. Studies show that allicin can help to protect against heart disease, diabetes, and some cancers, and it is also antibacterial and antifungal, warding off infections of the gut.

Interestingly, while the vitamin levels in many stored fruit and vegetables decrease over time, levels of alliin actually increase during storage, which is great news for gardeners who wish to keep their garlic bulbs for use over winter and early spring.

The plant not only protects our health, but it's delicious too, adding a spicy piquancy to a wide range of savoury dishes, while simply spreading crushed cloves on a slice of buttered toast will offer a quick fix of nutrients.

Growing garlic is easy if you have a sunny area with free-draining soil. Plant the cloves in autumn or winter for a summer harvest, since the crop needs a period of cold for the bulbs to develop. Set individual cloves 15cm (6in) apart with the pointed tips about 2.5cm (1in) below the soil surface. For more information on planting, harvesting and storing garlic, visit rhs.org.uk and search for "growing garlic".

If you don't have much space outside, try growing garlic shoots by submerging the base of peeled bulbs just below the surface in a jar of water. Roots soon form and the flavoursome shoots then appear from the top.

Barbados aloe

ALOE VERA

Benefits
Leaves help to heal burns

Height & spread
60 x 60cm (24 x 24in)

***Aloe vera* is an easy-care houseplant with a superpower that makes it indispensable for any household. This spiky succulent hails from the Middle East, where it has long been used as a treatment for burns and skin conditions.**

The plant will make you happy if you scald yourself on a hot cup of tea, or sit outside in the sun for too long, a quick application of the gel inside the leaf bringing instant relief. The gel contains various compounds that help to treat burns, including sunburn, promoting skin growth and repair. For this reason, aloe vera is often included in cosmetic skin creams and after-sun lotions, but before use, test a tiny amount on your skin to ensure you don't suffer an allergic reaction.

One of the plant's active ingredients is the chemical acemannan, which in research studies has also been shown to have antiviral properties that may help in the treatment of HIV, influenza and measles. Aloin, the yellow-brown compound lining the insides of the leaf, is a powerful laxative and another ingredient that may have use as a drug to treat cancer and brain injuries. However, aloin is toxic when ingested, and while the gel inside the leaf is not harmful, it is wise to wash your hands thoroughly after applying it to your skin.

Products containing aloe vera extract or gel are generally safe for most people, but always consult your GP before using them if you are pregnant or taking other medications.

Growing aloe vera is very easy: all it needs is a pot with a drainage hole at the bottom and some peat-free compost formulated for cacti and succulents. Place the potted plant on a sunny windowsill, moving it a little further away from the sun in summer, and water sparingly. Reduce watering in winter, giving it just enough to prevent the leaves from shrivelling.

False bishop's flower

AMMI MAJUS

Benefits
Wildlife plant (food for birds); seeds used to treat skin disorders

Height & spread
Up to 1.2 x 0.5m (48 x 20in)

This elegant annual flower is a relative of the carrot, and its edible leaves and seeds have been used in traditional medicine for millennia to treat a range of health problems.

A native of the Mediterranean region, *Ammi* makes us happy on many levels, forming a frothy sea of white-domed flowerheads in summer, held on tall stems above small, divided leaves, which can be cut for a vase display indoors.

In traditional medicine, a tincture of honey and the powdered seeds of *Ammi majus* was used to treat vitiligo, an autoimmune disorder that causes a loss of melanin and white patches to appear on the skin. Its healing properties are due to compounds in the seeds known as furanocoumarins, and it continues to be used today in medications to treat psoriasis, eczema and vitiligo.

However, care should be taken because bishop's flower can cause skin to become extra sensitive to the sun, and it is unsafe to eat the plant when you are pregnant or breastfeeding. Always consult your doctor before eating the seeds or leaves or using herbal products derived from *Ammi majus*, since they may cause side effects in some people and react with other medications.

The plant is easy to grow from seed. Sow in pots or trays of peat-free seed compost indoors in early spring, or *in situ* outside later in the season, and plant in full sun or part shade and free-draining soil. The tall plants will need staking in windy sites. Bishop's flower is hardy and birds enjoy the seeds.

Dill

ANETHUM GRAVEOLENS

Benefits
Wildlife plant (food for birds); contains flavonoids that protect against disease

Height & spread
1.2 x 0.5m (48 x 20in)

An easy-to-grow herb, dill produces leaves and seeds that have a sweet, slightly aniseed flavour which adds a tangy quality to a range of savoury dishes. Its delicate taste is enough to make it a happy plant, while its use in traditional medicine to relieve upset stomachs adds to its appeal.

Dill is a decorative herb, with blue-green ferny foliage and pretty, flat-topped, yellow flowerheads, loved by pollinators, and edible seeds that birds enjoy. Stems of dill also make attractive cut flowers.

A relative of carrots and celery, dill contains chemicals that may help to relax muscles, which is why it is thought to alleviate stomach cramps and menstrual pain, although, as yet, there is not enough scientific evidence to prove that it is effective in either case. However, dill is packed with flavonoids (see also p.55), which have been shown to help reduce the risk of heart disease and stroke, and other studies suggest that it can help to manage diabetes or even prevent it from developing.

Eating dill as a flavouring is generally safe, but consuming large quantities may cause skin to become extra sensitive to the sun, and it is unsafe to eat too much of the plant when pregnant. Always consult your doctor before using herbs or herbal products as medicines, since they may cause side effects, especially if you are taking other medications or have an allergy to the plants.

Sow dill seeds in pots and trays of peat-free seed compost indoors in early spring and plant out the seedlings in free-draining soil and full sun after the frosts have passed. A sheltered spot is best, too, since this tall herb can be battered by strong winds.

Pot marigold

CALENDULA OFFICINALIS

Benefits
Pollinator plant; flowers have antiseptic properties

Height & spread
50 x 30cm (20 x 12in)

This cheerful little flower is a popular choice for summer containers, its daisy-like orange flowers helping us to relax. The edible petals can be added to cooked rice, sprinkled on salads or used to colour mayonnaise, earning it the name poor man's saffron.

Research studies also show that pot marigold has antiseptic and anti-inflammatory properties, and topical cream with marigold extract was found to make skin look firmer and more hydrated. It has long been used to help heal wounds, too, and research shows that calendula ointment can reduce swelling and the healing time for Caesarean scars.

In *Grow Your Own Drugs*, James Wong cites other studies showing that when the petals are infused in water to make tea, they can help to relieve stomach aches and ulcers.

Check labels to make sure you are buying pot marigolds (*Calendula*) and not French marigolds, which are different plants, known as *Tagetes patula* (see pp.32–3), and use it sparingly at first, as the flowers may cause an allergic reaction in some people. Also, do not eat *Calendula* when pregnant or breastfeeding, and check with your doctor first if you are taking other medications.

Sow the seeds of this hardy annual in spring in pots or trays of peat-free seed compost, or directly *in situ* in a sunny or partly shaded spot and free-draining soil. Transfer seedlings in pots into raised beds or containers filled with peat-free potting compost. Alternatively, buy young plants in spring.

Deadheading the blooms regularly will promote a longer flower display for you and pollinators such as bees to enjoy.

Chamomile

CHAMAEMELUM NOBILE

Benefits
Pollinator plant; contains anti-anxiety compounds

Height & spread
25 x 25cm (10 x 10in)

Many people will have a packet of chamomile tea at home and enjoy the soothing benefits it can offer, while the plant from which the drink is derived can be grown in the garden, where its flowers offer similar relaxing effects.

Chamomile is a spreading perennial with finely divided, aromatic leaves and white daisy-like flowers. It can be grown as a lawn, where the crushed leaves release an apple-like fragrance when you walk on them, or plant it in beds and pots for its pretty blooms.

While chamomile's relaxing properties are well-known, *Chamaemelum nobile* is also a traditional remedy for toothache, stomach aches and headaches. Studies have not yet identified exactly which compound in the plant is responsible for its relaxing properties, but the flavonoid apigenin is a likely contender, as it is thought to reduce anxiety and calm the mind.

To make the relaxing tea, harvest the flowers fresh or pick stems and hang them upside down in a cool place to dry. Place either fresh or dried blooms in a tea diffuser or empty tea bag and steep in hot water for five to ten minutes, then remove the flowers.

Do not drink more than a cup or two of chamomile tea a day when pregnant or breastfeeding and check with your doctor before consuming it if you are taking other medications. Some people may also be allergic to this plant.

The perennial *Chamaemelum nobile* is the most commonly grown species, but you could also try German chamomile (*Matricaria recutita*), an annual with similar flowers used to make teas, which can be sown from seed in spring.

If you want to grow a chamomile lawn and enjoy the relaxing fragrance but not the flowers, opt for *Chamaemelum nobile* 'Treneague'. For teas, try *C. nobile* 'Flore Pleno' and plant it in containers of peat-free potting compost or in free-draining soil in a sunny or partly shaded spot. Both common chamomile cultivars are available as plug plants in spring.

Purple coneflower

ECHINACEA PURPUREA

Benefits
Pollinator plant; wildlife plant (food for birds); flowers protect against disease and promote good skin health

Height & spread
Up to 90 x 0.45m (36 x 18in)

The elegant purplish-pink flowers of this perennial coneflower, which adorn the garden for many weeks from midsummer to early autumn, have long been used in traditional remedies to ward off infections.

Native Americans first discovered the power of echinacea and used it to help boost immunity against illness, while modern science also provides evidence that it offers this and other health benefits.

Research studies show that the plant has anti-inflammatory, antioxidant and antiseptic properties, and it is thought to strengthen the immune system and reduce symptoms of colds and flu. Although it is still not known exactly which compounds in the plant produce this effect, it is thought that two chemicals, polysaccharides and glycoproteins, help to initiate an immune response.

The plant is also used for its antiseptic properties and creams and ointments containing echinacea can be applied to help heal wounds and treat eczema.

Supplements to boost your immunity are generally safe for most people but consult your doctor before using them if you are pregnant, breastfeeding or taking other medications.

To make echinacea tea, add ½ teaspoon of fresh flowers or cleaned and chopped roots to a tea diffuser or empty tea bag and steep in hot water for five minutes, then remove the plant part before serving.

To grow purple coneflower, buy young plants in spring and plant them in full sun and moist but well-drained soil. *Echinacea purpurea* is fully hardy and the flowers also attract pollinators, while birds eat the seeds and the seedheads offer a habitat for overwintering insects.

Mexican fleabane

ERIGERON KARVINSKIANUS

Benefits
Pollinator plant; plants may help to relieve cold and flu symptoms

Height & spread
15 x 30cm (6 x 12in)

The tiny white and pink daisy-like flowers of the Mexican fleabane help us to relax and make us happy, while its blooms and little green leaves are also thought to have health-boosting properties.

The plant's name derives from its use by Native Americans to deter unwanted insects such as fleas, but it is also used in traditional remedies as a diuretic and in the treatment of headaches, fevers and kidney problems. The crushed leaves are applied to cuts and wounds to promote healing, too. While the scientific evidence to support these health claims is not conclusive, some studies have shown that the plant has antimicrobial properties which ward off infections, making it a candidate for further research.

You can make a tea from the leaves and flowers, which may help to soothe the symptoms of colds and flu, by placing them in a tea diffuser or empty tea bag and steeping them in hot water for five minutes.

While Mexican fleabane is safe to drink or use as topical treatment for most people, consult your doctor before using it medicinally, and if you are pregnant or breastfeeding, or taking other medications. Some people may also be allergic to the plant.

Mexican fleabane is a very accommodating perennial and given free-draining soil and a sunny position, it will quickly self-seed to produce frills of semi-evergreen foliage covered with delicate white daisies that turn pink as they age. Sow the seed initially *in situ* outside or in pots or trays of peat-free seed compost in spring. The flowers are a good source of nectar for bees and other pollinators.

Meadowsweet

FILIPENDULA ULMARIA

Benefits
Pollinator plant; wildlife plant (food for birds); plants contain salicylates that help relieve pain

Height & spread
90 x 60cm (36 x 24in)

Meadowsweet, with its tall stems of fluffy white summer flowers, is used in traditional therapies to relieve pain and the symptoms of rheumatism and arthritis.

The claims about the plant's health benefits are borne out by scientific studies, which show that it contains chemicals called salicylates, which are similar to aspirin. Meadowsweet also contains polyphenols called ellagitannins, which have anti-inflammatory properties.

To make a soothing tea from the plant, harvest the flowers on a sunny day and hang them upside down indoors in a cool room to dry for two to three weeks. Then pop a few dried blooms into a tea diffuser or empty tea bag and steep in hot water for five to ten minutes, before removing the plant parts.

However, take care when using meadowsweet. While tea made from the plant is safe to drink occasionally, do not consume it regularly or if you have an allergy to aspirin. It is also best to avoid this plant if you are pregnant or breastfeeding, or if you are taking other medications.

Meadowsweet is a hardy perennial herb and a good choice for areas of heavy clay or moisture-retentive soil that may be unsuitable for other herbs. Buy plants in spring or autumn and plant in full sun or part shade.

The flowers also provide nectar for a range of pollinators, and birds enjoy the seeds, while the leaves offer food for the larvae of many moth species.

Fennel

FOENICULUM VULGARE

Benefits
Pollinator plant; wildlife plant (food for birds); contains potassium, calcium and magnesium; aids digestion and protects against disease

Height & spread
1.8 x 0.6m (6 x 2ft)

This tall herb, with its feathery leaves and tasty seeds, adds an aniseed flavour to salads, pasta and bread, and it is also used in traditional remedies to aid digestion and prevent heartburn, bloating, stomach cramps and constipation.

In fact, fennel has been used as a laxative for thousands of years, and studies show that it contains chemicals that help to relax the muscles in the colon, which produce the beneficial effects. In addition, it contains an ingredient that may act like the female hormone oestrogen, and there is evidence that it can help to relieve menstrual cramps and some symptoms of menopause, although studies are, as yet, inconclusive. Other research shows that fennel may increase the flow of breast milk in breastfeeding mothers.

Fennel also contains potassium, calcium and magnesium, which may help to lower blood pressure and protect against heart disease.

To make fennel tea and reap the digestive benefits of this herb, place one to two teaspoons of fennel seeds in a cup of boiling water and steep for five to ten minutes, then strain to remove the seeds. Reheat the tea to the desired temperature.

The herb is safe to consume as an ingredient in culinary dishes and in tea for most people, but consult your doctor before consuming it regularly if you are pregnant or taking other medications. Some people may also have an allergy to the plant.

Buy young plants of this hardy perennial herb in spring or sow seeds in moist but well-drained or free-draining soil – it's not too fussy – and full sun. The herb self-seeds easily, so you will probably find seedlings popping up elsewhere in the garden the following year. The heads of small yellow flowers attract pollinators and birds feast on the seeds that follow.

Benefits
Contains iron and rutin that helps alleviate depression

Height & spread
Up to 90 x 60cm (3 x 2ft)

Daylilies are beautiful ornamental plants that brighten up the garden with their trumpet-shaped flowers, which appear in succession over many weeks in summer, but did you also know that some plants are edible and used as a remedy for insomnia?

Daylilies' anti-inflammatory and antioxidant properties are well documented, and the flavonoid rutin, found in the flowers, has benefits for mental health, helping to alleviate depression and promote sleep by increasing the feel-good chemicals serotonin and dopamine in the brain.

Another study shows that the similar yellow-flowered *Hemerocallis citrina* may have anti-cancer properties, and research is ongoing into its health benefits. The flowers are also used in China to help relieve the pain of childbirth.

All parts of the daylily are edible, and the flowers have a delicate, sweet taste and are good sources of iron and dietary fibre, which improves gut health, as well as carotenoids (see also p.123) and vitamin A (see p.102). The nutritious roots can also be eaten and act as a mild laxative – try them as a substitute for potatoes.

However, take care before eating any daylilies, as research shows that only the orange species *Hemerocallis fulva* and yellow *Hemerocallis citrina* are safe to consume, and red cultivars may not be. The common lily (*Lilium*) species and cultivars are also harmful when ingested, so check plant labels very carefully, and consult your doctor before eating *Hemerocallis* if you are pregnant, breastfeeding or taking other medications. The plant is toxic to pets, too.

To grow this hardy perennial, plant it in full sun or part shade and moist but well-drained soil. The flowers last for only one day, hence the name, but appear in succession over many weeks, so they are ideal for picking and adding to your culinary dishes. You can dig up the roots in autumn, too, and since the plant self-seeds freely, the seedlings should compensate for harvested plants.

St John's wort

HYPERICUM PERFORATUM

Benefits
Pollinator plant; contains chemicals that help to heal wounds and alleviate symptoms of mild depression

Height & spread
90 x 60cm (3 x 2ft)

Toxicity
All parts are mildly toxic

This easy-care deciduous shrub, with its clusters of sunny yellow flowers, has been used in folk medicine for centuries to treat burns, bruises and other wounds, while the Ancient Greeks grew it to treat nervous disorders such as depression.

Recent research studies back up the traditional uses of St John's wort and show that the flowers, leaves and oil extracted from it have antibacterial properties, while the same chemicals that help to heal wounds are also thought to be responsible for its antidepressant effects.

It is believed that the chemicals hyperforin and hypericin are the active ingredients. These increase feel-good chemicals, including serotonin and dopamine, in the brain, resulting in improved mood and mental health, and extracts from the shrub are now used in a range of drugs and supplements to treat mild depression.

While the extracts are popular, all parts of the plant are mildly poisonous and only the flowers and young leaves can be consumed in small quantities after cooking or in teas. They also have side effects such as increased skin photosensitivity, increasing the risk of sunburn. Always consult your doctor before using the plant medicinally, especially if you are pregnant, breastfeeding or taking other medications. Some people may also have an allergy to the plant.

To grow this hardy shrub, plant it in a sunny or partly shaded site in moist but well-drained soil. After it is established, it requires little aftercare apart from a trim in spring, if it has outgrown its allocated space.

Peppermint

MENTHA × PIPERITA

Benefits
Good for pollinators; helps to aid digestion and improve memory

Height & spread
60 x 60cm (24 x 24in)

We are all familiar with the unique taste of peppermint, used in toothpaste and to freshen breath, as well as a flavouring in teas, confectionery, and sweet and savoury dishes.

Helping to lift our mood, the invigorating scent of peppermint is associated with renewal and energy, while research studies show that chemicals in the plant can enhance concentration and improve memory – evidence suggests that inhaling essential oil made from it improves learning.

The herb has also been used in folk medicine for hundreds of years to aid digestion, soothe stomach aches and treat nausea and vomiting, and modern science backs up these health claims, showing that it has anti-allergic, antifungal and antibacterial effects. Studies also show that peppermint can help to treat irritable bowel syndrome (IBS).

While few people have an allergy to peppermint and it is generally safe to consume in food and teas, peppermint oil may cause irritation and rashes when applied to the skin and it should not be used on the face.

As well as the flavoursome leaves, peppermint plants also produce spikes of tiny, pale purple flowers in late summer, which are loved by pollinators, while birds such as goldfinches eat the seeds.

This vigorous, hardy perennial herb is remarkably easy to grow, but it is best confined to a large pot of its own, and grown in peat-free soil-based compost, as it will soon swamp ornamentals and crops if planted out in the garden. It is happiest in part shade, although pots of mint will grow in full sun, if you are prepared to water them regularly.

Bergamot

MONARDA DIDYMA

Benefits
Pollinator plant; contains thymol, an antiseptic agent; aids digestion

Height & spread
90cm x 45cm (26 x 18in)

The beautiful tufted red flowers of bergamot brighten up the garden in summer, while the plant has been used for centuries in traditional remedies to treat a multitude of ills, including colds, headaches and nausea.

Both the flowers and leaves are edible, and Native Americans steeped upper parts of the species, *Monarda fistulosa*, in boiling water to make tea to relieve cold symptoms. They also used it to heal wounds, a treatment confirmed by scientific studies that show bergamot is a natural source of the antiseptic agent, thymol. The leaves can be made into a poultice to heal cuts, and bergamot is an active ingredient in many modern mouthwash products.

Bergamot tea is thought to aid digestion, too. The leaves and flowers act as a diuretic and help to relieve symptoms of flatulent colic and sickness. Other studies show that the essential oil, when used in aromatherapy, may help to improve learning and memory, but more research is needed to confirm these beneficial effects.

Both fresh and dried flowers and the leaves have a beneficial effect on health, and can be made into a soothing tea by placing them in a tea diffuser or empty tea bag and steeping in hot water for five minutes, before removing the plant parts. For most people, bergamot is safe to consume, but consult your doctor before using it medicinally if you are pregnant, breastfeeding or taking other medications. Some people may also be allergic to the plant.

Grow this hardy perennial plant in full sun or light, dappled shade and a moisture-retentive soil – it may suffer from powdery mildew disease in drier conditions.

Rose geranium

PELARGONIUM 'GRAVEOLENS'

Benefits
Scented foliage; oil from foliage promotes good skin health; helps protect against disease

Height & spread
20 x 30cm (8 x 12in)

The rose geranium belongs to the same group of plants as bedding geraniums (*Pelargonium*) and earns its place in this chapter because the leaves have a range of medicinal properties.

The foliage of this diminutive perennial has long been used in traditional remedies to treat cardiovascular, dental, gastrointestinal and respiratory disorders. Recent studies suggest that when inhaled, the essential oil from *Pelargonium* 'Graveolens' may, indeed, help to lower blood pressure and heart rate, although, as yet, there is insufficient evidence to prove its effectiveness conclusively.

Rose geranium's antiseptic and antifungal properties are well documented, and when the oil is made into a balm it can help to soothe eczema and other skin conditions. The active ingredients in the plant are citronellol and geraniol, both of which have healing properties, and research is now being conducted to see if the plant could also be used as a natural alternative to chemical food preservatives.

The plant is a tender South African evergreen perennial, often grown as an annual in cooler climes, and both the flowers and leaves are edible. The species has lemon-scented foliage, while cultivars such as 'Rose' smell of roses and are used to flavour desserts, teas and vinegars.

While the rose geranium is safe to eat in small quantities by most people, consult your doctor first if you are pregnant, breastfeeding or taking other medication. Some people may also have an allergy to the plant.

Buy young plants in late spring, and plant this tender perennial outside when all risk of frost has passed. It thrives in full sun or light shade and well-drained soil or peat-free compost in a container. Water well while the plants are establishing, after which they are very drought-tolerant; bring them indoors over winter.

Benefits
Contains vitamins K and A; promotes good skin, eye and gut health; protects against disease

Height & spread
45 x 45cm (18 x 18in)

PETROSELINUM CRISPUM

Used to flavour fish and other savoury dishes and to freshen breath, parsley is packed with vitamins and minerals that help to promote good health, while the leaves' high iron and folic acid content make them a useful treatment for anaemia.

Parsley is also a very good source of vitamin K, which helps blood clot and enhances bone strength, as well as vitamin A and the carotenoids lutein and zeaxanthin that enhance skin and eye health. Studies have shown that the herb's antimicrobial properties may help in the treatment of acne, too, and the flavonoids it contains, including apigenin, could protect against some cancers.

The herb has long been used to treat digestive disorders, and fibre in the leaves and stems helps to maintain good gut health, while their natural diuretic properties reduce bloating and relieve constipation.

Parsley is a nutritious herb, but consult your doctor before consuming very large quantities if you are pregnant, breastfeeding or taking other medications.

There are two common types of parsley – the flat-leaved or French variety and the curly-leaved variety. Both are from the same species, *Petroselinum crispum*, and offer the same health benefits. The herb is officially a biennial, which means it germinates and grows leaves in the first year and flowers and sets seed in the second. However, it is normally grown as an annual because, although it is hardy and can be overwintered, the leaves become coarser in the second year.

Sow seeds in pots or trays of peat-free compost in spring or buy young plants and set them outside in moist but well-drained soil in full sun or partial shade, or in a container filled with peat-free potting compost.

Self-heal

PRUNELLA VULGARIS

Benefits
Pollinator plant; contains rutin that helps alleviate depression; protects against infections and disease

Height & spread
30 x 30cm (12 x 12in)

This pretty, wild herb often pops up in the garden unannounced, its spikes of hooded purple flowers drawing pollinators throughout summer and early autumn, while the plant's name conveys its power to heal cuts and bites.

Self-heal has been used in folk medicine for centuries to treat other problems, too, including sore throats, intestinal infections and high blood pressure. It contains a number of flavonoids, including rutin, shown in recent research to help alleviate depression (see also p.165), and tannins, which have antioxidant, anti-allergic and antimicrobial properties that may help to ward off infections.

Other studies suggest that the herb's anti-inflammatory chemicals may help to prevent age-related diseases such as heart disease and some cancers, and though more research is needed to confirm these effects, it could offer potential as a resource for modern drugs.

All parts of self-heal are edible, and the young leaves can be added to salads or steamed as a green vegetable. The leaves can also be used to make herbal tea by placing them in a tea diffuser or old tea bag and steeping them in hot water for five to ten minutes, or make them into a salve to apply to wounds or insect bites.

Self-heal is safe to eat for most people, but consult your doctor before consuming very large quantities if you are pregnant, breastfeeding or taking other medications.

Either sow the seeds of this hardy perennial in pots or trays of peat-free seed compost in spring or buy young plants. Plant in full sun or part shade and moist but well-drained soil, although it is not very fussy and may grow in other conditions, too.

Feverfew

TANACETUM PARTHENIUM

Benefits
Pollinator plant; may protect against disease

Height & spread
60 x 30cm (24 x 12in)

Feverfew's daisy-like flowers and apple green, lobed leaves are reasons enough to grow this pretty herb, while its use in traditional therapies to reduce pain and fevers may also entice you.

The common name comes from the Latin word *febrifugia*, which means "driving away fevers", and it is used in herbal medicine to treat headaches and migraines and to reduce a high temperature. There is some scientific evidence to support its effectiveness in treating these complaints, but the results so far have been mixed.

However, the flowers and fruits that follow them contain a chemical called parthenolide, which recent studies have shown may have anti-cancer properties, and it is currently being tested in cancer clinical trials. Research into the plant as a potential treatment for arthritis and neuropathy is also being investigated.

The leaves of feverfew have a slightly bitter taste and can be added to salads or made into tea, while the dried flowers are used to flavour pastries. To make feverfew tea, place the leaves in a tea diffuser or old tea bag and steep in hot water for five to ten minutes.

While the herb is safe for most people, consult your doctor before ingesting it if you are pregnant, breastfeeding or taking other medications. Some people may also have an allergic reaction to the plant.

As well as its potential health benefits, feverfew will attract pollinators, such as bees and butterflies, and the aromatic foliage also repels some troublesome insects such as wasps and flies, so set a bowl of leaves on the dining table outside as a deterrent.

Feverfew is a hardy perennial herb and can be grown from seed in spring in pots or trays of peat-free seed compost, or sow directly into well-drained soil in a sunny site. It is a prolific self-seeder, so remove the flowers promptly if you don't want it to spread.

Benefits
Pollinator plant; has antiseptic properties; aids digestion, relieves pain and respiratory problems; promotes good skin health

Height & spread
Up to 20 x 40cm (8 x 16in)

Used to flavour a range of savoury dishes, thyme is a much-loved garden herb that deserves a place in any garden or in a pot on a patio or windowsill, while its use as an antiseptic is equally valuable but often overlooked.

The leaves contain a chemical called thymol, which relaxes the stomach muscles to improve digestion, prevent menstrual cramps and relieve respiratory problems. It also has antimicrobial properties and is used in deodorants and mouthwashes, and in dentistry to treat infections.

When made into a salve, thyme can help to soothe skin and relieve eczema symptoms, while oil made from the herb helps to relieve aching muscles and the effects of rheumatism. To make thyme oil, fill a sterilized jar with the leaves and cover them with olive or almond oil, then leave to steep for at least two weeks. Do a patch test on your skin to ensure you don't react to the herb oil before adding a few drops to a bath. Essential oil made from thyme is also available to buy.

Thyme is a happy plant for all these reasons and because it is a wonderful pollinator plant, attracting bees and butterflies to its nectar-rich flowers in summer.

This herb is generally safe to eat for most people, although you should consult your doctor if you plan to use the oil medicinally, especially if you are pregnant, breastfeeding or taking other medications. Some people may also be allergic to the plant.

Grow this dwarf evergreen shrub from seed in pots or trays of peat-free seed compost in spring, or buy young plants. Plant it in a sunny or partly shaded spot and free-draining soil. Clip the plant with shears after flowering to keep it bushy.

Fenugreek

TRIGONELLA FOENUM-GRACECUM

Benefits
Contains vitamins A, C, and K; promotes good eye, skin and heart health; may protect against disease

Height & spread
25 x 25cm (10 x 10in)

This unassuming herb may be a new one to many people, but it's a key ingredient in many Asian dishes such as curries and pickles, and used as a flavouring for bread and cheese. It also has a long history of use in traditional medicine, mainly to aid digestion and relieve constipation.

More recent scientific studies show that fenugreek comes with a whole package of health benefits. Research has shown that it has anti-diabetic properties, regulating the production of enzymes that control blood sugar levels, and helps to reduce "bad" cholesterol and improve cardiovascular health.

Several studies have shown that the plant can protect against cancer, too, and some even suggest that it may have a role in treating some forms of the disease by helping to shrink tumours. Its antibacterial and antifungal properties are other benefits, and research is ongoing into its ability to fight drug-resistant infections. Supplements containing the herb are also sold as a remedy for menstrual cramps.

In addition, fenugreek is a rich source of iron and calcium, which protect against anaemia and promote healthy bones, as well as vitamins A, C and K, which contribute to eye, skin and heart health.

While the plant is safe when eaten in food, consult your doctor before consuming larger quantities if you are pregnant, breastfeeding or taking other medications.

Fenugreek is not grown widely in Europe, but it is definitely worth setting aside a space for this leafy annual in your garden. The leaves have a delicious earthy flavour that sweetens when cooked, and the seeds smell and taste like maple syrup.

Sow the seeds in a sunny spot and free-draining soil outside in spring. It can also be used as a green manure to protect the soil.

Home comforts

Bringing plants into your home is a great way to enjoy their benefits all year round, particularly in the short days of winter, while some have specific features that have been shown to lift our mood and make us smile.

Spider plant

CHLOROPHYTUM COMOSUM

Benefits
Decorative foliage; increases oxygen levels

Height & spread
Up to 12 x 60cm (12 x 24in)

One of the easiest houseplants to grow, the much-loved spider plant has decked the shelves of many a student apartment and new home, delivering colour and joy, in exchange for a minimal amount of care.

Research by the RHS shows that healthy houseplants boost mental wellbeing by reducing stress and improving our mood, and because spider plants are so easy to care for, they make a great choice when spirits need lifting.

This easy-going plant is very beautiful, too, with its fountains of green, or green and white striped, strappy foliage, and baby plantlets, or "spiders", that dance around it on long, pale cream arching stems.

Like all houseplants, this cheerful beauty also increases oxygen levels, a blessing within an indoor living space, and it is non-toxic to humans and pets, making it perfect for any family home.

The little spiders that dangle from the stems can bring you happiness, too. Simply remove these baby plants and pop the bases into jars of clean water. When they form roots, pot them up in peat-free compost and gift them to family and friends. The satisfaction of making new plants is uplifting, while this act of kindness is guaranteed to bring a smile to the faces of the recipients.

Spider plants thrive in some shade – close to an east- or north-facing window will suit them perfectly – and peat-free compost. Keep the compost moist during the growing period from spring to autumn, and reduce watering in winter, giving just enough to prevent the plant from wilting. The biggest threat to a spider plant is over-pampering. Take care not to water too much by planting it in a pot with drainage holes in the bottom and watering over the sink, leaving it to drain before replacing the pot in a waterproof container. Feed with a balanced liquid fertilizer every two to three weeks from mid-spring to early autumn to keep it healthy.

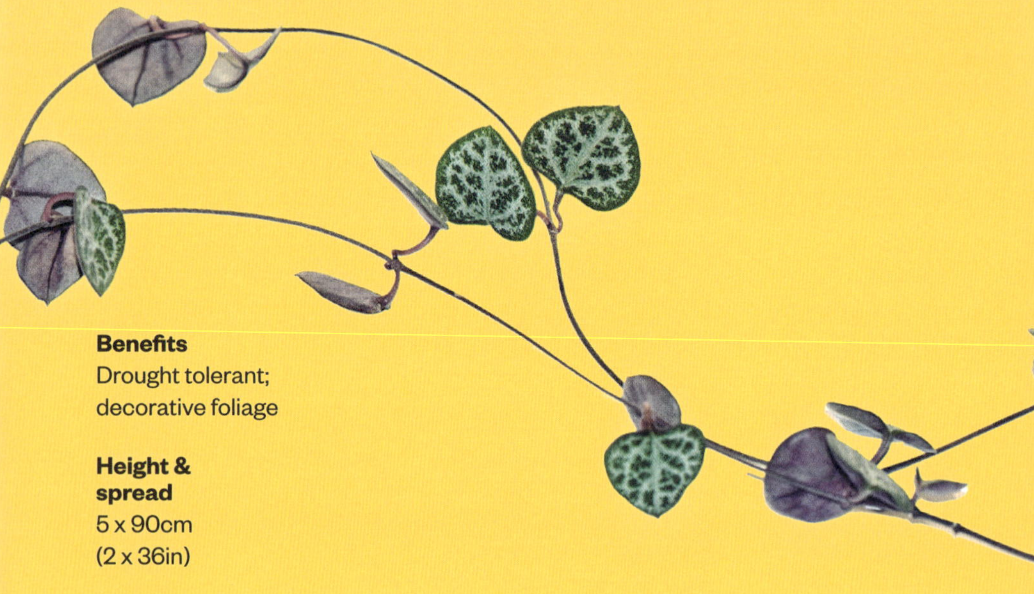

Benefits
Drought tolerant; decorative foliage

Height & spread
5 x 90cm
(2 x 36in)

String of hearts

CEROPEGIA LINEARIS SUBSP. *WOODII*

Nature's little gift of love, this trailing evergreen perennial, with its slender stems of tiny, patterned, heart-shaped leaves, is tougher than it looks, sailing through weeks of neglect.

Hailing from Africa, string of hearts is very drought-tolerant and makes a beautiful addition to a small hanging basket. Its stems can reach over 2m (6ft 6in) in length – simply trim the ends if they get too long – and the dainty foliage is grey-green with cream markings and purple undersides. In summer, small pink and purple tubular flowers appear, followed by long seedpods.

Keep it thriving by placing it in full sun and watering only when the top of the compost feels dry. Reduce watering in winter, giving just enough to prevent the leaves from shrivelling. Feed with a half-strength balanced fertilizer every fortnight in summer.

Areca palm

CHRYSALIDOCARPUS LUTESCENS

Benefits
Calming, round shape; decorative foliage

Height & spread
2 x 1m
(6 x 3ft)

Also known as the bamboo palm, this large, handsome houseplant is a joy to own, according to a recent research study by RHS Science and the University of Reading.

The study focused on 12 plants and asked participants to identify their favourites. The areca palm was voted one of the top three plants, its rounded shape and large, decorative leaves, which made them feel calm and promoted a positive response. It also evoked images of holidays and tropical destinations.

Not only is the areca palm highly decorative, it's also quite easy to care for. Place the plant in a bright spot, out of direct sunlight, and water when the top of the compost feels dry, ideally using rainwater or distilled water. This palm likes a humid atmosphere, and will enjoy life in a bathroom or kitchen, if those rooms also offer sufficient sunlight for its needs. Opening windows during the warmer months and standing the plant pot on a tray of damp pebbles will also increase the atmospheric humidity. You may find this palm for sale under its former name, *Dypsis lutescens*.

Venus fly trap

DIONAEA MUSCIPULA

Benefits
Fascinating foliage

Height & spread
10 x 20cm
(4 x 8in)

A guaranteed talking point, the carnivorous Venus fly trap is an intriguing plant, loved by adults and children alike. Its trick is to lure flying insects into its toothed, jawlike foliage traps, which then snap shut, imprisoning the unsuspecting victim inside.

The plant's enzymes then break down the insect and digest it. This grizzly operation is fascinating and holds our attention, allowing our brains to relax and reboot (see also p.50), while the green and red traps create a decorative display.

The Venus fly trap's spectacular performances make it a tempting purchase, but it requires special care to thrive. A swamp dweller in its native habitat, it likes permanently wet soil, and is best planted in a pot filled with perlite and a substrate made from sustainably produced sphagnum moss. Stand the pot in a saucer of rainwater or distilled water – it will baulk at hard tap water – removing it in winter but still keeping the plant moist. It prefers full sun and temperatures of 10–27°C (50–80°F); ideally move it to a slightly cooler room in winter. Do not add fertilizer and don't be tempted to drop other objects or even dead flies into its traps, as it will suffer if forced to perform too often.

Golden pothos

EPIPREMNUM AUREUM

Symbols
Drought- and shade-tolerant foliage

Height & spread
2 x 2m (6ft 6in x 6ft 6in)

Toxicity
All parts are toxic

The trailing pothos produces long stems of lush foliage that can cascade from a hanging basket or be trained up a mossy pole, while participants in a study by RHS Science and the University of Reading (see also p.189) said they loved its colour and shape.

The pothos's rounded shape, eye-catching gold and green heart-shaped foliage and trailing habit stole the show in the research study and it was voted one of the top three on the participants' list of favourite houseplants (12 plants were surveyed in the study).

It is also possibly the easiest of all houseplants to grow, thriving on neglect and gaining its other common name, devil's ivy, because it is almost impossible to kill and can survive periods in darkness. The trick is not to overwater it – only irrigate when the top of the compost feels dry – and to place it out of direct sunlight. You can apply a balanced liquid fertilizer every month from spring to autumn, but it will not suffer much if it's fed less frequently.

Weeping fig

FICUS BENJAMINA

Benefits
Calming rounded shape; decorative foliage

Height & spread
Up to 3.5 x 1.2m (10 x 4ft)

Toxicity
All parts are toxic

The elegant weeping fig is a tall, leafy houseplant that will make a statement in any home that can accommodate it. A favourite in the research study by the RHS and University of Reading (see also p.189), this sophisticated plant was one of the top three participants liked the best.

Described as the most beautiful by many people in the study, researchers said that this plant also made participants feel uplifted and relaxed.

The weeping fig has a long, clear main stem, often plaited, and a canopy of small, glossy leaves that are either green or green and cream variegated, which can be trimmed into a pleasing sphere or columnar shape. Keeping it healthy is also key to the happiness you will derive from this fig or, indeed, any houseplant, since a sickly plant could have the opposite effect on your mood.

While it is not especially fussy, it will thrive when given a position out of strong, direct sunlight and away from radiators. Water with tepid rainwater or distilled water, allowing the top of the compost to dry out between applications, and keep the compost just moist in winter. Set the plant on a tray of damp pebbles and open the windows during the warmer months to increase humidity levels. Applying a half-strength liquid fertilizer once a month from spring to early autumn will also help to keep it happy.

Once your weeping fig is in a position that suits it, try not to move it, which may cause the leaves to drop – often very rapidly. Because mature plants are expensive, it is a good idea to buy a smaller plant and experiment to see which areas of your home it prefers.

Variegated snake plant

SANSEVIERIA TRIFASCIATA

Benefits
Drought- and shade-tolerant decorative foliage

Height & spread
75 x 30cm (30 x 12in)

Toxicity
All parts are toxic

Also known as mother-in-law's tongue, this striking, drought-tolerant house plant is one of the easiest to grow, thriving on neglect and happy in some shade. For these reasons alone, owning one can help to make us happy.

Sporting slim, spiky, dark and pale green variegated stems, the snake plant sails through long periods of drought unscathed, and thrives in sun or light shade. Research shows that healthy plants make us happy and since this one is so easy to keep in pristine condition, it's a great choice for anyone wishing to enjoy the benefits in their home.

Houseplants such as the snake plant have been shown to reduce stress levels when we gaze at them, improving our mood, and, in some studies, they were also shown to increase attention span. So, it is definitely worth keeping one or two plants close to your desk, either at home or in the office.

Scientific studies also suggest that the snake plant has the potential to reduce Volatile Organic Compounds (VOCs), chemicals emitted from some furnishings, detergents, and paints that can have adverse effects on our health, although the research is not conclusive.

More recent studies have shown that proteins in the snake plant may be able to slow down the movement of cancer cells, and certain compounds it contains could be helpful in the treatment alopecia. However, do not be tempted to consume it, as all parts of the plant are toxic.

Growing a snake plant couldn't be easier: use cactus compost and plant it in a pot with drainage holes in the base, ensuring the leaves are not submerged beneath the surface. From spring to autumn, water your plant over a sink when the top layers of compost feel dry, and leave it to drain before placing it in a waterproof container to display in your home. Also apply a half-strength balanced liquid fertilizer once a month. In winter, stop feeding and reduce watering, applying just enough to prevent the foliage from shrivelling.

Peace lily

SPATHIPHYLLUM WALLISII

Benefits
Decorative foliage; calming flowers

Height & spread
Up to 60 x 60cm (24 x 24in)

Toxicity
All parts are toxic

The peace lily is a popular houseplant and it's easy to see why it has so many admirers. Not only is it almost bullet-proof and easy to care for, the handsome flowerheads last for many months, while the glossy green leaves have a pleated texture and offer interest when it's not in bloom.

The plant's simple, pale-coloured flowers are made up of a white petal-like spathe (modified leaf) surrounded by a creamy yellow spadix, and research shows that they aid relaxation. It blooms from spring to early autumn, and the flowers turn pale green as they start to fade, creating a duotone effect.

The benefits of this beautiful plant are not just aesthetic, either, and research by the RHS and University of Birmingham shows that it can reduce levels of the pollutant nitrogen dioxide from the air by up to 20 per cent. This gas is emitted from car fumes, and the burning of other fossil fuels such as coal and natural gas. The additional oxygen emitted by the peace lily and other houseplants also helps to increase our concentration levels (see also p.169).

As for the peace lily's care, nothing could be easier. Place your plant out of direct sunlight and away from radiators. Standing it on a tray of damp pebbles and opening the windows during the warmer months to increase humidity levels will also keep it happy, although it's not too demanding and is unlikely to suffer, unless the air in your home is very dry. Water when the top of the compost feels dry – plants will also tell you when they need a drink because the foliage may wilt, but it soon perks up once it is watered.

Wear gloves when trimming the stems, as the sap can cause skin irritation.

Fern arum

ZAMIOCULCAS ZAMIIFOLIA

Benefits
Drought- and shade-tolerant foliage

Height & spread
Up to 90 x 80cm (36 x 32in)

Toxicity
All parts are toxic

Also known as the ZZ plant, the fern arum will make you happy because it is beautiful and needs little maintenance, making it ideal for time-poor plant parents. Research also shows that it can help to remove polluting nitrogen dioxide from the air.

Hailing from eastern Africa, the fern arum is drought-tolerant and copes with low light and low humidity levels. While it may not be the most glamorous houseplant, it is perfect for adding height and structure to a group display, producing a vase-shaped cluster of tall stems punctuated with pairs of small, glossy, dark green leaves.

If you are lucky, it may also produce arum-like green and white flowers, similar to those of a peace lily (see also pp.196–7), at the base of the stems in summer, followed by white berries. The blooms often appear when the plant is slightly stressed, so check that it is not ready to be repotted.

The popularity of the fern arum – which is not actually a fern but a tropical herbaceous perennial – is partly due to its ability to thrive on neglect. Place it in a warm room in some shade and out of direct sun, and water only when the top of the compost feels dry. Also apply a half-strength balanced liquid fertilizer once a month from spring to autumn. Take care to avoid overwatering your plant, which is probably the only way you can kill it. Prevent soggy compost by planting it in a pot with drainage holes in the base and water it over a sink, then leave it to drain before replacing it in a waterproof container. Alternatively, stand large specimens on a deep saucer and tip any excess water away after irrigating. Follow these steps and you will have a happy, healthy plant, which RHS research shows will lift your mood and make you happy too.

Bibliography

*All websites accessed on 3–6 October 2025

Agatonovic-Kustrin, S., Morton, D. (2018) *Studies in Natural Products Chemistry* [Online] Available at: https://www.sciencedirect.com/topics/chemistry/parthenolide#:~:text=Melanomas%20are%20generally%20hard%20to,cancer%20cells%20killed%20after%20radiotherapy

Ahmadi, F., Pourghorban, A., Kharghani, S. *et al.* (2020) *The Effect of Fennel and Black Seed, on Breast milk, Prolactin Levels and Anthropometric Index in Human and Animal Samples: A Review.* [Online] Available at: https://jpp.mums.ac.ir/article_15053_e0defd621cdefb9a7aae1aa141fcd48e.pdf

Al-Mijalli, S., Mrabti, H *et al.* (2022) *Chemical Profiling and Biological Activities of Pelargonium graveolens Essential Oils at Three Different Phenological Stages.* [Online] Available at: https://pmc.ncbi.nlm.nih.gov/articles/PMC9459842/#:~:text=Among%20several%20P.,pharmacological%20activities%20and%20PGEO%20compounds

Alam, T. (2014) *Incredible Health Benefits of Solanum lycopersicum: A Point of View.* [Online] Available at: https://www.researchgate.net/publication/371071553_Incredible_Health_Benefits_of_Solanum_lycopersicum_A_Point_of_View

Arvinte, O.M., *et al.* (2023) *Rowanberry—A Source of Bioactive Compounds and Their Biopharmaceutical Properties. Section 7: Conclusion.* [Online] Available at: https://pmc.ncbi.nlm.nih.gov/articles/PMC10536293/#sec7-plants-12-03225

Bakowska-Barczak, A., Kolodziejczyk, P. (2011) *Black currant polyphenols: Their storage stability and microencapsulation.* [Online] Available at: https://www.sciencedirect.com/science/article/abs/pii/S0926669010002475#:~:text=Black%20currant%20berries%20are%20excellent,2006%2C%20Neto%2C%202007)

Barnhart, M. (2019) *Cleaning up Chernobyl with Sunflowers.* [Online] Available at: https://athensscienceobserver.com/2019/05/16/sunflowers-to-the-rescue/

Belho, N., *et al.* (2022) *Phytochemical screening and antimicrobial activity of Erigeron karvinskianus DC.* [Online] Available at: https://www.plantsjournal.com/archives/2022/vol10issue5/PartA/10-5-7-680.pdf

Berger, M *et al.* (2021) *The Influence of air pollution on pollen allergy sufferers* [Online] Available at: https://pmc.ncbi.nlm.nih.gov/articles/PMC8638356/

Dreher, D. (2018) *Surprising Research on the Color Blue* [Online] Available at: https://www.psychologytoday.com/gb/blog/your-personal-renaissance/201810/surprising-research-on-the-color-blue

Ellis, L. (2025) *Brighten up 'Blue Monday' – Research shows that the colour blue is not all gloom* [Online] Available at: https://student.sussex.ac.uk/news/article/66860-brighten-up-blue-monday-research-shows-that-the-colour-blue-is-not-all-gloom

Gatta, F., Mitchell, K. (2024) *Health Benefits of Echinacea.* [Online] Available at: https://www.webmd.com/diet/health-benefits-echinacea

Goodarzi, M., *et al.* (2016) *The Role of Anethum graveolens L. (Dill) in the Management of Diabetes.* [Online] Available at: https://pmc.ncbi.nlm.nih.gov/articles/PMC5088306/#:~:text=AG%20has%20many%20useful%20effects,in%20glucose%20and%20lipid%20pathways

Griffin, R., Ferdinand, P., Mitchell, K. (2023) *What Is Chamomile?* [Online] Available at: https://www.webmd.com/diet/supplement-guide-chamomile

Griffin, R., Watson, S. (2024) *Everything About Aloe Vera.* [Online] Available at: https://www.webmd.com/diet/supplement-guide-aloe-vera

Griffiths, A., Allaway, Z., Keightley, M., Gatti, A. (2020) *Your Wellbeing Garden, p97 and p.110.* London: DK.

Guo, Y., *et al.* (2022) *Protective effect of Monarda didymaL. Essential oil and its main component of thymol on learning and memory impairment in aging mice. Section 5: Conclusion.* [Online] Available at: https://pmc.ncbi.nlm.nih.gov/articles/PMC9464920/#s5

Harries, B., Chalmin-Pui, L. S., Gatersleben, B., Griffiths, A., & Ratcliffe, E. (2024). *Identifying features within a garden linked to emotional reactions and perceived restoration. Cities & Health, p.1–13.* [Online] Available at: https://doi.org/10.1080/23748834.2023.2300235

He, X., *et al* (2020) *Passiflora edulis: An Insight Into Current Researches on Phytochemistry and Pharmacology.* [Online] Available at: https://pmc.ncbi.nlm.nih.gov/articles/PMC7251050/

Hong, S., *et al.* (2018) *Aloe vera Is Effective and Safe in Short-term Treatment of Irritable Bowel Syndrome: A Systematic Review and Meta-analysis.* [Online] Available at: https://pmc.ncbi.nlm.nih.gov/articles/PMC6175553/#:~:text=It%20has%20been%20shown%20to%20have%20hepato%2Dprotective%2C,as%20a%20substance%20to%20improve%20gastrointestinal%20motility

Hossain, M., Touby, S. (2020) *Ammi majus an Endemic Medicinal Plant: A Review of the Medicinal Uses, Pharmacological and Phytochemicals.* [Online] Available at: https://pdfs.semanticscholar.org/0a8b/c6d6c0fb9452c1dc1cee9e1f1a48d1393d7a.pdf

Igwe, E., Charlton, K. (2016) *A Systematic Review on the Health Effects of Plums (Prunus domestica and Prunus salicina)* [Online] Available at: https://pubmed.ncbi.nlm.nih.gov/26992121/#:~:text=Plums%20have%20been%20shown%20to,Prunus%20domestica%20/%20chemistry*

Janda, K., *et al.* (2020) Passiflora incarnata *in Neuropsychiatric Disorders—A Systematic Review.* [Online] Available at: https://pmc.ncbi.nlm.nih.gov/articles/PMC7766837/#:~:text=Passiflora%20incarnata%20is%20one%20of%20the%20herbal%20remedies%20used%20to,disorders%20of%20the%20nervous%20system

Jaradat, N., Hawash, M *et al.* (2022) *Chemical Markers and Pharmacological Characters of Pelargonium graveolens Essential Oil from Palestine.* [Online] Available at: https://pmc.ncbi.nlm.nih.gov/articles/PMC9457828/#:~:text=Pelargonium%20graveolens%20leaves%20are%20widely,Candida%20albicans%20compared%20with%20Fluconazole

Kalola, U., Patel, P., Nguyen, H. (2024) *Galantamine* [Online] Available at: https://www.ncbi.nlm.nih.gov/books/NBK574546/

Karakaş, F *et al.* (2011) *The evolution of topical administration of Bellis perennis fraction on circular excision wound healing in Winstar albino rats* [Online] Available at: https://www.tandfonline.com/doi/full/10.3109/13880209.2012.656200#:~:text=Discussion%20and%20conclusion:%20Topically%20administered,verified%20for%20the%20first%20time

Kew (2025) *Dracaena trifasciata: Snake plant.* [Online] Available at: https://www.kew.org/plants/snake-plant

Khalil, N., *et al.* (2020) *Ammi Visnaga L., a Potential Medicinal Plant: A Review.* [Online] Available at: https://pmc.ncbi.nlm.nih.gov/articles/PMC7024292/#:~:text=The%20decoction%20and/or%20powdered,7%2C8%2C9%5D

Landete, J.M. (2011) *Ellagitannins, ellagic acid and their derived metabolites: A review about source, metabolism functions and health.* [Online] Available at: https://www.sciencedirect.com/science/article/abs/pii/S0963996911002572#:~:text=Biological%20effects%20of%20ellagitannins%2C%20ellagic,anti%2Dinflammatory%20and%20prebiotic%20effects

Li, P., *et al.* (2023) *Research on the anti-ageing mechanism of Prunella vulgaris L. Section 21: Conclusion.* [Online] Available at: https://www.nature.com/articles/s41598-023-39609-1#Sec21

Lillehei, A., Halcón. L., Savik, K., Reis, R. (2015) *Effect of Inhaled Lavender and Sleep Hygiene on Self-Reported Sleep Issues: A Randomized Controlled Trial* [Online] Available at: https://pmc.ncbi.nlm.nih.gov/articles/PMC4505755/#:~:text=A%20small%20

to%20moderate%20benefit,specific%20to%20lavender%20and%20sleep.&text=Lavender%20(Lavandula%20angustifolia)%20essential%20oil,18%20and%20its%20safety%20profile

Lin, S., *et al.* (2013) *The Antidepressant-like Effect of Ethanol Extract of Daylily Flowers in Rats.* [Online] Available at: https://pmc.ncbi.nlm.nih.gov/articles/PMC3924984/#:~:text=Daylily%20flower%20(%E9%87%91%E9%87%9D%E8%8A%B1%20J%C4%ABn,antidepressant%2Dlike%20effects%20of%20DFEtoH

Lv, X., *et al.* (2022) *Effects of Peppermint Essential Oil on Learning and Memory Ability in APP/PS1 Transgenic Mice.* [Online] Available at: https://pmc.ncbi.nlm.nih.gov/articles/PMC9000406/#:~:text=Evidence%20suggests%20that%20peppermint%20aroma,of%20serum%20AchE%20%5B13%5D

Mahboubi, M. (2016) *Rosa damascena as holy ancient herb with novel applications.* [Online] Available at: https://www.sciencedirect.com/science/article/pii/S2225411015000954#:~:text=The%20modern%20investigations%20on%20R,ear%20pain%20and%20hemmorroid%20ailments.&text=full%2Dsize%20image-,Fig.,the%20results%20of%20these%20researches

Marshall, B. (2020) *Grow Yourself Healthy: Gardening to transform your gut health all year round.* London: Frances Lincoln

Masubuchi, R., Watanabe, S., Satou, T. (2019) *Effects of Inhalation of Geranium Essential Oil on Blood Pressure and Heart Rate in Mice.* [Online] Available at: https://journals.sagepub.com/doi/full/10.1177/1934578X19881534

Meeran, M., *et al.* (2017) *Pharmacological Properties and Molecular Mechanisms of Thymol: Prospects for Its Therapeutic Potential and Pharmaceutical Development.* [Online] Available at: https://pmc.ncbi.nlm.nih.gov/articles/PMC5483461/#:~:text=Thymol%20improves%20digestion%20by%20relaxing,et%20al.%2C%201998)

Mikstas, C. (2024) *Health Benefits of Aronia Berries* [Online] Available at: https://www.webmd.com/diet/health-benefits-aronia-berries

Mikstas, C. (2025) *Health Benefits of Mint Leaves.* [Online] Available at: https://www.webmd.com/diet/health-benefits-mint-leaves

Mosley, M. (2023) *Just One Thing: Cook tomatoes to boost their health benefits.* [Online] Available at: https://www.bbc.co.uk/programmes/articles/f9Lq0ljbMt1H4Cm061yCYF/michael-mosley-cook-tomatoes-to-boost-their-health-benefits#:~:text=Drinking%20tomato%20juice%20has%20also,inflammation%20markers%20in%20their%20blood

Moss, M., *et al.* (2017) *Any Sense in Classroom Scents? Aroma of Rosemary Essential Oil Significantly Improves Cognition in Young School Children. Advances in Chemical Engineering and Science 07, 450–463.*

Murray, M. (2020) *Textbook of Natural Medicine (Fifth Edition), Vol. 1 Antiviral Effects.* [Online] Available at: https://www.sciencedirect.com/topics/medicine-and-dentistry/acemannan#:~:text=Antiviral%20Effects,weeks%20after%20termination%20of%20treatment.&text=At%20the%20end%20of%20the,influenza%20virus%2C%20and%20measles%20virus

Nam, H., Nan, L., Choo, B. (2021) *Anti-Inflammation and Protective Effects of Anethum graveolens L. (Dill Seeds) on Esophageal Mucosa Damages in Reflux Esophagitis-Induced Rats. Section 1: Introduction.* [Online] Available at: https://pmc.ncbi.nlm.nih.gov/articles/PMC8535990/#sec1-foods-10-02500

Nathan, P. (2001) *Hypericum perforatum (St John's Wort): a non-selective reuptake inhibitor? A review of the recent advances in its pharmacology.* [Online] Available at: https://pubmed.ncbi.nlm.nih.gov/11277608/#:~:text=Although%20the%20major%20constituent%20responsible,a%20direct%20or%20indirect%20role

National Center for Complementary and Integrative Health (2025) *Valerian.* [Online] Available at: https://www.nccih.nih.gov/health/valerian#:~:text=Today%2C%20valerian%20is%20promoted%20for,are%20used%20for%20medicinal%20purposes

National Center for Complementary Health (2025) *Fenugreek.* [Online] Available at: https://www.nccih.nih.gov/health/fenugreek#:~:text=Fenugreek%20is%20a%20clover%2Dlike,foods%2C%20beverages%2C%20and%20tobacco

National Center for Complementary Health (2025) *Ginkgo.* [Online] Available at: https://www.nccih.nih.gov/health/ginkgo

Northumbria University (2016) *Herbs that can boost your mood and memory.* [Online] Available at: https://www.northumbria.ac.uk/about-us/news-events/news/2016/04/herbs-that-can-boost-your-mood-and-memory/

Olennikov, D., Kashchenko, N., Chirikova, N. (2016) *Meadowsweet Teas as New Functional Beverages: Comparative Analysis of Nutrients, Phytochemicals and Biological Effects of Four Filipendula Species.* [Online] Available at: https://pmc.ncbi.nlm.nih.gov/articles/PMC6155584/#sec4-molecules-22-00016

Perry, N.S.L., *et al.* (2018) *A randomised double-blind placebo-controlled pilot trial of a combined extract of sage, rosemary and melissa, traditional herbal medicines, on the enhancement of memory in normal healthy subjects, including influence of age.* [Online] Available at: https://www.sciencedirect.com/science/article/abs/pii/S0944711317301046

Plants For A Future (2000) *Pinus sylvestris - L.* [Online] Available at: https://pfaf.org/user/Plant.aspx?LatinName=Pinus+sylvestris

Plants For A Future (2025) *Hemerocallis fulva – L. Medicinal Uses.* [Online] Available at: https://pfaf.org/user/plant.aspx?LatinName=Hemerocallis+fulva#:~:text=Medicinal%20Uses&text=The%20flowers%20are%20anodyne%2C%20antiemetic,a%20blood%20purifier%5B240%5D

Plants For A Future (2025) *Monarda didyma – L. Medicinal Uses.* [Online] Available at: https://pfaf.org/user/Plant.aspx?LatinName=Monarda+didyma#:~:text=Medicinal%20Uses&text=The%20leaves%20and%20flowering%20stems,disorders%5B4%2C%20238%5D

Rahbardar, M.G., Hosseinzadeh, H. (2020) *Therapeutic effects of rosemary (Rosmarinus officinalis L.) and its active constituents on nervous system disorders. Section 3: Conclusion.* [Online] Available at: https://pmc.ncbi.nlm.nih.gov/articles/PMC7491497/#sec3

Rather, M., *et al.*. (2016) *Foeniculum vulgare: A comprehensive review of its traditional use, phytochemistry, pharmacology, and safety.* [Online] Available at: https://www.sciencedirect.com/science/article/pii/S1878535212000792#s0110

RHS (2025) *Hedge your bets with 'super plant' to fight air pollution* [Online] Available at: https://www.rhs.org.uk/science/articles/super-cotoneaster

RHS (2025) *Houseplants: to support human health.* [Online] Available at: https://www.rhs.org.uk/plants/types/houseplants/for-human-health

RHS Lindley Collections (2025) *Healing Garden: A History of Medicinal Plants.* [Online] Available at: https://www.rhs.org.uk/digital-collections/healing-garden

Saddique, Z., Naeem, I., Maimoona, A. (2010) *A review of the antibacterial activity of Hypericum perforatum L.* [Online] Available at: https://www.sciencedirect.com/science/article/abs/pii/S0378874110005131#:~:text=The%20sole%20antibacterial%20principle%20isolated,far%20are%20hyperforin%20and%20hypericin

Salehi, B *et al.* (2018) *Tagetes spp. Essential Oils and Other Extracts: Chemical Characterization and Biological Activity* [Online] Available at: https://pmc.ncbi.nlm.nih.gov/articles/PMC6278309/

Saqib, S., *et al.* (2022) *Mentha: Nutritional and Health Attributes to Treat Various Ailments Including Cardiovascular Diseases.* [Online] Available at: https://pmc.ncbi.nlm.nih.gov/articles/PMC9572119/

Science Direct (2025) *Chokeberry* [Online] Available at: https://www.sciencedirect.com/topics/agricultural-and-biological-sciences/chokeberry#:~:text=Chokeberry%20has%20the%20highest%20content,with%20C4%20C6%20and%20C4

Science Direct (2025) *Pelargonium Graveolens* [Online] Available at: https://www.sciencedirect.com/topics/agricultural-and-biological-sciences/pelargonium-graveolens

Science Direct (2025) *Witch-Hazel* [Online] Available at: https://www.sciencedirect.com/topics/medicine-and-dentistry/witch-hazel

Shah, M *et al.* (2022) *Pharmacological and medicinal value of Jasmine* [Online] Available at: https://www.researchgate.net/publication/368987901_PHARMACOLOGICAL_AND_MEDICINAL_VALUE_OF_JASMINE

Sidor, A., Gramza-Michałowska, A. (2015) *Advanced research on the antioxidant and health benefit of elderberry (Sambucus nigra) in food – a review* [Online] Available at: https://www.sciencedirect.com/science/article/pii/S1756464614002400#:~:text=Elderberry%20has%20medicinal%20properties%20associated%20with%20the,on%20blood%20pressure%2C%20glycaemia%20reduction%2C%20immune%20system

Tan, S. (2024) *What Are the Health Benefits of Marigold Extract (Calendula)?* [Online] Available at: https://www.webmd.com/vitamins-and-supplements/what-health-benefits-marigold-extract-calendula

Tan, S. (2024) *What are the Health Benefits of Oyster Mushrooms?* [Online] Available at: https://www.webmd.com/diet/what-health-benefits-oyster-mushrooms

Tesfaye, A. (2021) *Revealing the Therapeutic Uses of Garlic (Allium sativum) and Its Potential for Drug Discovery. Section 5: Conclusion.* [Online] Available at: https://pmc.ncbi.nlm.nih.gov/articles/PMC8739926/#sec5

Traverso, V. (2020) *Urban trees can help cut air pollution from New York to Beijing, but which trees do the best job?.* [Online] Available at: https://www.bbc.co.uk/future/article/20200504-which-trees-reduce-air-pollution-best

University of Surrey (2024) *Being rough and hairy isn't all it's cracked up to be – at least if you're a tree.* [Online] Available at: https://www.surrey.ac.uk/news/being-rough-and-hairy-isnt-all-its-cracked-be-least-if-youre-tree

Vanbuskirk, S., Mitchell. K. (2024) *Health Benefits of Chili, Chili Peppers, and Chili Powder.* [Online] Available at: https://www.webmd.com/diet/health-benefits-chili-peppers

Varshney, H., Siddique, Y. (2023) *Medical Properties of Fenugreek: A Review.* [Online] Available at: https://openbiologyjournal.com/VOLUME/11/ELOCATOR/e187503622302220/FULLTEXT/#:~:text=Trigonella%20foenum%20graecum%20(fenugreek)%20belongs,DNA%20adduct%20formation%20%5B4%5D

Venkatachalam, K., *et al.* (2023) *Phytochemicals, Bioactive Properties and Commercial Potential of Calamondin (Citrofortunella microcarpa) Fruits: A Review.* [Online] Available at: https://pmc.ncbi.nlm.nih.gov/articles/PMC10146261/

Verma, P. (2015) *Lemon Balm (Melissa officinalis L.) An herbal medicinal plant with broad therapeutic uses and cultivation practices: A review* [Online] Available at: https://www.researchgate.net/publication/285581177_LEMON_BALM_MELISSA_OFFICINALIS_L_AN_HERBAL_MEDICINAL_PLANT_WITH_BROAD_THERAPEUTIC_USES_AND_CULTIVATION_PRACTICES_A_REVIEW

Wang, H. (2023) *Beneficial medicinal effects and material applications of rose, section 5: Conclusions* [Online] Available at: https://pmc.ncbi.nlm.nih.gov/articles/PMC10758878/#sec5

Waseem, M., *et al.* (2024) *Phytoremediation of heavy metals from industrially contaminated soil using sunflower (Helianthus annus L.) by inoculation of two indigenous bacteria.* [Online] Available at: https://www.sciencedirect.com/science/article/pii/S2667064X23001641

WebMD (2025) *Feverfew – Uses, Side Effects, and More.* [Online] Available at: https://www.webmd.com/vitamins/ai/ingredientmono-933/feverfew

WebMD (2025) *Garlic – Uses, Side Effects, and More.* [Online] Available at: https://www.webmd.com/vitamins/ai/ingredientmono-300/garlic

WebMD (2025) *Meadowsweet – Uses, Side Effects, and More.* [Online] Available at: https://www.webmd.com/vitamins/ai/ingredientmono-108/meadowsweet

Won Lee, H., *et al.* (2021) *Fennel (Foeniculum vulgare Miller) for the management of menopausal women's health: A systematic review and meta-analysis.* [Online] Available at: https://www.sciencedirect.com/science/article/abs/pii/S1744388121000591#:~:text=Fennel%2C%20also%20known%20as%20Foeniculum,management%20of%20menopausal%20women's%20health

Wong, J. (2009) *Grow Your Own Drugs*. Glasgow: Collins

Wong, J., *et al.* (2020) *Salvia sclarea L. Essential Oil Extract and Its Antioxidative Phytochemical Sclareol Inhibit Oxytocin-Induced Uterine Hypercontraction Dysmenorrhea Model by Inhibiting the Ca^{2+}–MLCK–MLC20 Signalling Cascade.* [Online] Available at: https://pmc.ncbi.nlm.nih.gov/articles/PMC7602146/#sec1-antioxidants-09-00991

Wu, M., Lui, L., Xing, Y., Yang, S., Li, H., Cao, Y. (2020) *Roles and Mechanisms of Hawthorn and Its Extracts on Atherosclerosis: A Review.* [Online] Available at: https://pmc.ncbi.nlm.nih.gov/articles/PMC7047282/

You, M., Zhao, L., Song, L. (2023) *A novel protein extracted from Hemerocallis citrina Borani inhibits hepatocellular carcinoma cell proliferation by regulating mitochondria-dependent apoptosis and aerobic glycolysis.* [Online] Available at: https://pmc.ncbi.nlm.nih.gov/articles/PMC10786776/#Sec15

Zelman, K. (2024) *Health Benefits of Green Beans.* [Online] Available at: https://www.webmd.com/diet/health-benefits-green-beans

Zelman, K. (2024) *Health Benefits of Parsley.* [Online] Available at: https://www.webmd.com/diet/health-benefits-parsley

Zholdasbayev, M., *et* al. (2023) *Prunella vulgaris L.: An Updated Overview of Botany, Chemical Composition, Extraction Methods, and Biological Activities.* [Online] Available at: https://pmc.ncbi.nlm.nih.gov/articles/PMC10460042/#sec7-pharmaceuticals-16-01106

The publishers would like to thank the following sources for their kind permission to reproduce the pictures in this book:

Adobe Stock: M88 195

RHS: Claude Aubriet 77, 90, 97; Richard Bloom 89; James Bolton 190; Mark Bolton 80; Sarah Cuttle 62; Paul Debois 13, 35; Simon Garbutt 127; Philippa Gibson 16; Susan Grayer 148; Wilf Halliday 66, 76; Paul Harris 15; Neil Hepworth 19, 41, 65, 91, 133, 144, 206; Joanna Kossak 47, 130, 196; Fiona Lea 163; Charlotte Maguire 69, 138; Barry Phillips 176; Katy Prentice 141; RHS, Herbarium 171; Karen Robbirt 107; Tim Sandall 61, 79, 108, 117, 121, 122, 151, 175, 180, 191, 199; Carol Sheppard 42, 46, 51, 75, 95, 152, 156, 159, 179; Sirastudio 27; Mike Sleigh 57, 137, 147; Nichola Stocken 23, 28, 86, 103, 104, 112, 134, 168; Graham Titchmarsh 20, 38, 48, 52, 160; Eleanor Walpole 31; Kat Weatherill 84; Christopher Whitehouse 24, 58; Mark Winwood 4, 7, 30, 83, 92, 164

Shutterstock: a4ndreas 71; AjayTvm 54; Alina Bitta 100; Olesia Bech 155; Esin Deniz 172; Irisha_S 33; Irkhabar 96; Orest lyzhechka 125; JNix 34; Jaroslav Machacek 111; Alex Manders 45; Alex Maschtakov 193; Morphart Creation 14; Olena758 188; Pixel-Shot 189; Manfred Ruckszio 167; Liliya Shlapak 124; TuktaBaby 186; Hayat Ullah5599 183; Iva Vagnerova 70; Yankane 11; Mei Yi 55; Tania Zbrodko 118

Index

First published in 2026 in association with
The Royal Horticultural Society by Welbeck
An Imprint of HEADLINE PUBLISHING GROUP LIMITED

1

Cataloguing in Publication Data is available from the British Library

ISBN 9781035428717

Printed and bound in China

Headline's policy is to use papers that are natural, renewable and recyclable products and made from wood grown in well-managed forests and other controlled sources. The logging and manufacturing processes are expected to conform to the environmental regulations of the country of origin.

HEADLINE PUBLISHING GROUP LIMITED
An Hachette UK Company
Carmelite House
50 Victoria Embankment
London EC4Y 0DZ

The authorised representative in the EEA is Hachette Ireland,
8 Castlecourt Centre, Dublin 15, D15 XTP3, Ireland (email: info@hbgi.ie)

www.headline.co.uk
www.hachette.co.uk